Living in God

366 Themes for Daily Meditative Contemplation and Spiritual Enrichment

WITH LIFE-ENHANCING AFFIRMATIONS AND INSPIRATIONAL QUOTATIONS

ROY EUGENE DAVIS

D1313256

MOTILAL BANARSIDASS PUBLISHERS
PRIVATE LIMITED • DELHI

First Indian Edition: Delhi, 1998,
Reprint: Delhi, 2000

First Published in 1997 in USA

© 1997 BY ROY EUGENE DAVIS
All Rights Reserved.

ISBN: 81-208-1543-2 (Cloth)
ISBN: 81-208-1544-0 (Paper)

Also available at:

MOTILAL BANARSIDASS

236, 9th Main III Block, Jayanagar, Bangalore 560 011
41 U.A. Bungalow Road, Jawahar Nagar, Delhi 110 007
8 Mahalaxmi Chamber, Warden Road, Mumbai 400 026
120 Royapettah High Road, Mylapore, Chennai 600 004
Sanas Plaza, 1302 Baji Rao Road, Pune 411 002
8 Camac Street, Calcutta 700 017
Ashok Rajpath, Patna 800 004
Chowk, Varanasi 221 001

Printed in India
BY JAINENDRA PRAKASH JAIN AT SHRI JAINENDRA PRESS,
A-45 NARAINA, PHASE-I, NEW DELHI 110 028
AND PUBLISHED BY NARENDRA PRAKASH JAIN FOR
MOTILAL BANARSIDASS PUBLISHERS PRIVATE LIMITED,
BUNGALOW ROAD, DELHI 110 007

LIVING IN GOD

I salute the supreme teacher,
the Truth, whose nature is bliss;
who is the giver of the highest
happiness; who is pure wisdom;
who is beyond all qualities and
infinite like the sky; who is beyond
words; who is one and eternal,
pure and still; who is beyond all
change and phenomena and who
is the silent witness of all our
thoughts and emotions—I salute
Truth, the supreme teacher.

BOOKS BY ROY EUGENE DAVIS
Published by Motilal Banarsidass

Life Surrendered in God
With Commentary on Patanjali's yoga-sutras

A Master Guide to Meditation
and Spiritual Growth

The Book of Life

INTRODUCTION

The desire to know God is innate to every person. What is not commonly known is that, because God's being is the only reality in existence, every person, creature, and thing in nature is already abiding in God.

All souls are expressive units of God's consciousness. Cosmic forces emanating from God comprise the field of nature: our world. Living consciously in God only requires that we acknowledge the facts of life as they are, and train ourselves to be aware of God's presence all of the time. When we are grounded in right understanding, and choose to learn by experience how to be aware of what is true about ourselves in relationship to the Infinite, spiritual growth is progressive and satisfying and our lives are made orderly and meaningful by our own right endeavors and the redemptive actions of God's grace.

My purpose for publishing this book is to encourage readers to nurture their soul qualities and fully awaken to and experience the highest good of which they are capable in all aspects of their lives. Some of the themes are selections from my previous writings; others are new.

In the text, the word *Self*, when spelled with an upper case *S*, is used to refer to our true nature as individualized expressions of God's consciousness. When we clearly experience the difference between our essential nature as pure consciousness and ordinary, conditioned states of awareness, we are Self-realized. When we are more spiritually awake and actually know and vividly experience the reality of God, we are God-realized. When we are God-realized and our innate knowledge is Self-revealed to the extent that we apprehend the full reality of God and understand the causative actions of consciousness, we are enlightened. When we are permanently enlightened, we are liberated from all erroneous beliefs and illusional perceptions which formerly clouded our awareness.

To benefit from this book, daily read a selection from the text, early in the morning if possible, and think about the theme during the day. An ideal time to read is immediately after an interlude of quiet prayer and meditation. The chosen selection can also be perused at night, just before going to sleep. It can be helpful to read aloud the themes, quotations, and affirmations. It can be beneficial to read the affirmations several times, until a definite shift of awareness is experienced.

ROY EUGENE DAVIS

Summer 1997
Lakemont, Georgia
U.S.A.

366 Themes for Daily Meditative Contemplation and Spiritual Enrichment

Meditating in the Sanctuary of the Soul

There is a quiet place within you to which you can retire whenever you desire to experience perfect peace and wholeness. Rest in conscious awareness of your true nature every day as you meditate in God.

•   Sit upright. Close your eyes. Direct your attention inward to the space between your eyebrows. Pray silently, or sit quietly for a few moments. You are a spiritual being abiding in the ocean of God's presence.

•   If meditation flows spontaneously, let it happen. If it does not, use a helpful meditation technique to elicit relaxation and mental calm: breath awareness, listening to a chosen word or word-phrase (mantra), or any procedure that you know to be helpful. Have no anxiety about the outcome of practice. Avoid effort. Remain attentive.

•   When you are poised and tranquil, rest in that calm, aware state until you feel inclined to conclude the practice session. Retain your meditative calm as you resume your activities. Be happy. Be thankful.

Meditate once or twice a day for fifteen to twenty minutes to refresh the mind, improve overall health, and facilitate natural spiritual growth. Meditate longer whenever you want to experience the deep silence of the soul.

There is an enlivening Power nurturing the universe
and we can learn to cooperate with it.

JANUARY

January 1

Until we are enlightened, we see only the surface of our world; we do not perceive or know about the subtle levels of nature, or *that* which produced them out of itself and sustains them. We need to know the truth about ourselves, our relationship with God, and how to live as we are meant to live.

January 2

Every soul desires to eternally exist in a condition of permanent, conscious happiness. This desire is compelling because of the soul's innate inclination to have its awareness restored to wholeness.

January 3

Our awareness is restored to wholeness when it is no longer clouded because of blind identification with thoughts, moods, and illusions. We then realize that God's consciousness is individualized as us.

Life has to be lived; why not live it the highest way?
— *Paramahansa Yogananda* —

January 4

Spiritual enlightenment cannot be compared to any self-conscious, egocentric state; it liberates soul consciousness, illumines the mind, imparts the radiance of health to the body, allows God's grace to flow, and harmoniously adjusts personal circumstances.

January 5

For our spiritual growth to be authentic, it is necessary that we be able to easily apply the knowledge that unfolds from within the depths of the soul.

January 6

On the awakening path, we do not have to struggle to become spiritually aware. The direct way to unfold innate capacities is to cooperate with the awakening processes already occurring within us, and to learn how to effectively live with the full support of nature.

Know you not that your body is the temple of the Holy Spirit?
— *New Testament / 1 Corinthians 6:19* —

January 7

Because we are individualized expressions of God's consciousness, all knowledge of God and of universal processes is within us and is Self-revealed to the extent that it is allowed to unfold. When we are fully aware of ourselves as immortal, spiritual beings, our capacity to know the reality of God is limitless.

January 8

God's omniscient, omnipotent, self-existing reality emanates the fields of space and time and expresses everything that is manifested. The word *god* is derived from the Indo-European language ancestor word *hu*, "the one who is invoked." God's transcendent aspect is nameless because formless and devoid of attributes.

January 9

The Oversoul aspect of God is the first objective manifestation from Supreme Consciousness: the Absolute, the field of pure Existence-Being. The reality of God expresses as the varied aspects of nature that we perceive and to which we relate.

Lead me from the unreal to the real! Lead me from
darkness to light! Lead me from [belief in] death to
[realization of] immortality!
—- *The Brihadaranyaka Upanishad* —

January 10

The field of primordial nature is manifested by Om, the Word, flowing from the Godhead. This vibratory force expresses as primordial nature: time, space, and cosmic particles with potential to further manifest. It is the substance of all that is expressed and formed as the universe. Om can be heard in the silence of meditation.

January 11

Primordial nature has two characteristics: it produces forms and it veils consciousness; it makes universal manifestation possible and clouds awareness of souls which are overly identified with it. Its forces are regulated by three constituent qualities that contribute to luminosity, transformation, and inertia.

January 12

God's consciousness is individualized when its light is reflected from the field of primordial nature. Because our individualized consciousness is the true Self of us, we are immortal. Complete knowledge of God and of cosmic processes is innate to us.

In the beginning was the Word [Om], and the Word was with God ... All things were manifested by it.
— *The Gospel According to Saint John 1:1& 3* —

January 13

Believing God to be omnipresent, omnipotent, omniscient, and supportive is comforting. It enables us to have faith that no matter how difficult or chaotic personal, social, or global conditions may be, God can and will eventually harmoniously adjust them so that everything will be brought to a satisfactory conclusion. Simple trust nurtures hope and elicits confidence until clear comprehension of the reality of God is acquired and realization replaces mere belief.

January 14

God is the first cause, the primary mover that produces effects. God, being self-complete, cannot be in need of improvement. As the reality of souls, God cannot be in need of further enlightenment.

January 15

The final solution to all human problems is spiritual enlightenment: knowledge of ourselves as spiritual beings abiding in God's wholeness.

In one verse I will tell you that which has been taught in thousands of scriptures. Brahman [the Absolute] is real, the world is illusory; the true Self is Brahman and nothing else.
— *Adi (the first) Shankara* —

January 16

Knowledge of God is beyond the grasp of ordinary powers of reason and intellect; it can be partially apprehended when intellectual skills are refined, and directly known when intuition is unrestricted. Intellectual skills are improved by using them, a sincere desire to learn, cultivating mental and emotional peace, nurturing physical health, and regular superconscious meditation practice. Intuition is enhanced by quieting the mind and senses.

January 17

While we need to relate effectively to the mundane realms and acquire knowledge that enables us to live comfortably, comprehending the reality of God is vital to our permanent happiness and well-being.

January 18

Belief is mental acceptance of or firm conviction about the actuality of something. Do we own our beliefs or are they owned by someone else? By passively agreeing with the opinions of others, we deny ourselves the joy and freedom that personal discovery provides.

I absorbed my attention within and realized my true Self.
— *Kabir* —

January 19

As sojourners in the cosmic ocean of life, we are fated to wander in time and space and to experience a variety of impermanent relationships and circumstances until, having discovered the truth about ourselves in relationship to the Infinite, we awaken from the dream of mortality and fulfill our spiritual destiny.

January 20

We experience fate, the effects of mental conditionings and personal actions, because of clouded awareness and conflicted mental and emotional states. Our destiny is fulfilled when we are in harmony with nature's rhythms and responsive to innate soul impulses and the redemptive actions of God's grace.

January 21

To be fulfilled we need to be in harmonious accord with the processes of nature, have life-enhancing desires easily fulfilled, have all needs spontaneously provided, and experience authentic spiritual growth that culminates in illumination of consciousness.

> The true Self is never born, nor does it die.
> The true Self is permanent and ageless.
> — *Bhagavad Gita 2:20* —

January 22

To mistake the unreal for the real is the primary intellectual error that results in irrational thinking and behaviors that reinforce the soul's addictions to mundane relationships and circumstances. Enlightened teachers recommend that fascination with transient phenomena be avoided. Attention and endeavors should be directed to awakening to Self-knowledge.

January 23

Sincere aspiration to spiritual growth, wisely chosen personal behaviors, and responsiveness to the soul's innate urge to have awareness restored to wholeness make soul unfoldment easier and rapid.

January 24

Are all of our purposes meaningful—of real value? It is not difficult to find something of interest to which to devote our time, energies, and resources. We need to inquire: When I have completed my projects, satisfied my desires, and fulfilled my commitments, will all of my actions have been worthwhile?

On this road [spiritual path], to abandon one's own way is to enter on the true way, to pass onwards to the goal; to forsake one's own way is to enter that which has none; namely God.
— *St. John of the Cross* —

January 25

A life that is not effectively lived with a clear sense of meaningful purpose is almost entirely wasted, and the soul's desire to be free is frustrated because awakening to illumination of consciousness—the primary reason for our having been born into this world—is neglected.

January 26

When we know how to live, are sustained by faith, and motivated and energized by our Self-confident will to excel, we can redeem the troubled past and be assured of continuous unfoldments of good fortune.

January 27

When we are Self-confident it is easy to be enthusiastic, enjoyable to envision desired outcomes of plans and actions, rewarding to see through appearances of discord to harmonious possibilities that can be actualized, pleasant to accept good fortune that is immediately available, and natural to have our highest good come into manifestation by concentrated intention, unwavering faith, and effective actions.

Your word is a lamp unto my feet and a light unto my path.
— *The Book of Psalms 119:105* —

January 28

We can discover the best way to live by effectively using our talents and abilities, being curious about and envisioning possibilities, engaging in soul-satisfying endeavors, praying for guidance, and being alert and responsive to the many worthwhile circumstances, events, and relationships life presents to us.

January 29

Any work we do, service we render, or action we perform that produces entirely constructive results is life-enhancing; it is beneficial to us and to others. When our relationships with the universe are harmonious, we are included in its processes and it satisfies our needs. Resources, supportive events, and circumstances are appropriately provided for our highest good.

January 30

We can and should always desire the highest good for others and, with faith, release that desire into Universal Mind. Whatever is impressed into Universal Mind can be expressed as objective circumstances.

If you desire something with concentrated intention, if it does not yet exist, the universe will manifest it for you.
— *Sri Yukteswar, guru of Paramahansa Yogananda* —

January 31

If immediate awakening to transcendence does not occur, an intentional way to allow the emergence of pure consciousness is to recognize and eliminate personal characteristics which are common to the spiritually unawake condition, some of which are:

• Lack of knowledge of the true nature of the Self.
• Errors in intellectual discernment (delusions) and inaccurate perceptions (illusions) of what is thought about, experienced, or observed.
• Confusion regarding the difference between pure consciousness and ordinary states of awareness.
• Obsessive identification with ego-awareness: the cause of our false sense of individuality.
• Strong attachment to pleasant experiences, or to beliefs, opinions, or personal circumstances.
• Anxiety or worry about the possibility of having painful experiences in the near or distant future.
• Preoccupation with fears of death, which may be instinctive, or nurtured by latent memories of past episodes of dying.

Affirmation

God's enlivening Spirit ever nurtures my
total well-being, effects necessary psychological
transformations, facilitates rapid spiritual growth,
and harmoniously adjusts relationships and
circumstances for my highest good.

How to Use Affirmations Effectively

Practice until you are proficient.

*   Be still, where you will not be disturbed.
*   Acknowledge your innate, divine nature.
*   Acknowledge God's Presence in and around you.
*   Speak the affirmation aloud, in a firm, clear voice, with alert intention and soul-felt conviction.
*   Repeat it aloud a few times. Let your awareness, thoughts, and feelings conform to the affirmation.
*   Affirm a few more times, in a quieter tone of voice.
*   Whisper it a few times; close your eyes and take it into your mind and consciousness.
*   Affirm mentally, taking the meaning of the affirmation deeply within and contemplating its essence.
*   Continue to calmly, mentally affirm until realization of the affirmation is obviously experienced.

Another way to effectively use affirmations:

*   Speak the affirmation aloud, with conviction, until your awareness and mental attitude changes; maintain those constructive states.
*   If you have difficulty staying with the process, stand in front of a mirror and observe yourself as you speak the affirmation with conviction. Stand tall. Be Self-confident, with quiet enthusiasm.

*I am a fully awake, vital, immortal spiritual
being superior to all circumstances.*

FEBRUARY

February 1

Spiritual growth occurs naturally when we live in harmony with nature's laws and aspire to know God.

February 2

To restore our awareness to wholeness we need to be able to discern the difference between our real, permanent nature as pure consciousness and the fragmented states of ordinary awareness commonly experienced when our attention is overly identified with mental and emotional states and sense perceptions. We can do this by calm Self-analysis and repeated practice of superconscious meditation.

February 3

Sitting to meditate every day is the certain way to remove awareness from personality-based limitations. When we are established in Self-knowledge and aware of our relationship with God, it is easy to successfully live with insightful understanding.

Every day, meditate more deeply than you did the day before.
— *Paramahansa Yogananda* —

February 4

Various ways of resisting, restraining, weakening, making dormant, and removing characteristics of ordinary awareness which obscure the soul's pure consciousness can be applied and practiced with benefit. These may include disciplined endeavor to regulate them, nonattachment, superconscious meditation practice, and other helpful supplemental practices.

February 5

Supplemental practices that unveil the true nature of the soul include the nurturing of faith along with persistent endeavor to facilitate spiritual growth, cultivation of devotion to God, commitment to the ideal of enlightenment, enhancement of intellectual and intuitive abilities, and wholesome lifestyle regimens to increase overall health and vitality.

February 6

Mastery of attention is necessary for rational thinking, focused concentration, effective living and success in meditation practice. Accomplish Self-Mastery.

Unregulated thought processes persist because of the restless movements of *pranas* [the soul's life forces].
— *Lahiri Mahasaya, guru of Sri Yukteswar* —

February 7

For harmonious relationships and psychological health and to weaken and subdue mental activities which blur awareness, the five *external* disciplines to be cultivated and perfected are (1) harmlessness; (2) truthfulness; (3) honesty; (4) conservation and transmutation of vital forces; (5) nonpossessiveness.

February 8

When neither thoughts nor inclinations to cause injury to ourselves, others, or anything in nature are present in our awareness, and when our actions are entirely constructive and nurturing, we are established in harmlessness. Inwardly peaceful, we are always on friendly terms with everyone and everything.

February 9

To be established in truthfulness is to know the truth about ourselves in relationship to God and nature and to live from that understanding. We can then skillfully and easily accomplish our worthwhile purposes.

Spiritual practices are implemented to eliminate all physical and mental obstacles for the purpose of realizing God.
— *Patanjali's yoga-sutras 2:2* —

February 10

It is natural for us to be honest in our relationships and interactions when we are true to ourselves and live responsibly with the knowledge that our thoughts, states of consciousness, and actions always determine our experiences because of our intimate relationship with God and God's omnipresent Mind.

February 11

Worry, anxiety, stress, restlessness, confusion, emotional distress, useless talking, addictive behaviors, insufficient rest, and excessive sensory stimulation dissipate vital forces, weaken the mind, and obscure soul awareness. Faith, optimism, relaxation, certainty, emotional calmness, decisiveness, wholesome behaviors, a balanced schedule of activity and rest, and regular interludes of prayer and meditation energize the mind, vitalize the body, and enhance spiritual awareness.

The devotee whose mind is disciplined, who moves in the world with the senses under control and who is free from attachments and aversions, is established in tranquility. That purity of spirit removes one from all sorrows. One's knowledge is [then] soon settled in permanent peace.
— *Bhagavad Gita 2:64,65* —

February 12

Mental and emotional detachment from fixed beliefs, material things, and transient circumstances liberates our awareness and allows us to see the world as it is—a play of cosmic forces in the Mind of God.

February 13

The five internal disciplines to be cultivated and perfected are (1) purity of thoughts and motives; (2) inner contentment in all circumstances; (3) psychological transformation by insightful self-analysis and elimination of addictive tendencies, self-defeating mental attitudes and habits, delusions, illusions, and irrational responses to memories; (4) meditation practice; (5) surrender of self-consciousness in favor of Self- and God-realization.

Lord, I want to be more holy in my mind. My thoughts tend ever to be divisive and scattered. In so many ways, my mind is a house divided; and the conflicts rage up and down all my corridors. I need wholeness. O that my mind may be stilled by thy holy hush! Lord, I want to be more holy in my mind.
— *Howard Thurman | Meditations of the Heart* —

February 14

When the mind is purified, thinking is orderly and rational. Then soul-impelled and wisdom-directed, our choices of actions and relationships are always clearly defined and constructively purposeful.

February 15

Regardless of mental or emotional conflicts to be resolved or of outer circumstances to be harmonized, we can choose to be soul-content. Knowing that material things—including the mind—are external to the soul, nothing need ever disturb our perfect peace.

February 16

Psychological conflict inhibits spiritual growth. To make spiritual growth easier, mental conditionings and emotional conflicts that restrict the soul's impulse to have awareness restored to wholeness should be removed. As soul awareness increases, superconscious influences complete the transformation processes.

To get at the core of God ... one must first get into
the core of the self ... Go to the depths of the soul, the
secret place of the Most High, to the roots, to the heights;
for all that God can do is focused there.
— *Meister Eckhart* —

February 17

Affirm with conviction: "I acknowledge that I am a spiritual being endowed with all of the characteristics and qualities of God. I see clearly, know truly, and live efficiently with knowledgeable, inspired purpose."

February 18

The illusional sense of independent selfhood is due to lack of spiritual awareness. When egocentric self-consciousness is discarded, pure soul awareness remains. Ignorance is replaced by knowledge. The full reality of God is flawlessly apprehended.

February 19

After quiet meditation, intently inquire, "What is the real nature of God?"; "What is my relationship to God?"; "What is my purpose for being in this world?"; "What can I do to know God and fulfill my spiritual destiny?"

By deep meditation and by living for God alone, calm the waves of thought and desire that constitute your present perception of reality. Then in superconsciousness, you will behold everything as it really is.
— *Paramahansa Yogananda* —

February 20

A devoted spiritual aspirant will not err in thinking the way—the lifestyle routines and meditation practices which facilitate spiritual growth—to be the goal itself. Nor will that devotee be attached to novel theories or meaningless activities which distract attention from being committed to psychological transformation and awakening to Self-knowledge.

February 21

A mind devoid of confusion, delusions, and illusions efficiently processes thoughts and sense-conveyed information and welcomes spontaneous unfoldments of the soul's innate knowledge. When Self-knowledge unfolds, it provides us a new perception of reality that illumines the mind, results in unrestricted flows of soul awareness, and allows spontaneous, wisdom-directed, effective, fulfilled living to be actualized.

This is the noble truth of the way which leads
to the stopping of sorrow. It is the noble eightfold
path ... right views, right aspirations, right speech,
right conduct, right livelihood, right endeavor, right
mindfulness, and right contemplation.
— *The teachings of the Buddha / The Pali Canon* —

February 22

When we are simultaneously aware of our egocentric desires and of soul-impelled inclinations, although we may want to perform constructive actions, conditioned behaviors may also be compelling. We may be aware of our virtuous qualities, yet be inclined to fulfill the impulses and urgings of the restless mind and the sensation-seeking senses. The solution is to use discriminative intelligence to make wise choices.

February 23

Affirmation: "Established in Self-realization, I make wise choices and skillfully perform right actions."

February 24

Inconvenient or uncomfortable circumstances can be patiently endured until knowledge of how to improve them is acquired. Patience is actualized when we are soul-centered, mentally peaceful, and emotionally calm regardless of circumstances.

The soul is immortal. God's attributes permeate the soul.
Let your spiritual path be that of God-communion.
— *Lahiri Mahasaya* —

February 25

When we are Self-realized, we are undisturbed by any outer condition. Evidence of our degree of spiritual awareness is our ability to remain insightfully poised in the face of challenge and discord.

February 26

When established in Self-knowledge, we are content and unconcerned about various philosophical or religious opinions or theories. When our intellect is purified, subtle truths are easily discerned and soul knowledge spontaneously unfolds of its own accord.

February 27

For the Self-realized devotee, no compulsory actions are performed; all actions are naturally impelled by the soul. Established in comprehensive understanding of life's wholeness, the devotee is nurtured and supported by the inexhaustible Source of everything.

In God I put my trust.
— *The Book of Psalms 11:1* —

February 28

To awaken to liberation of consciousness, our aspiration to experience it should be unwavering, supported by personal actions that ensure harmonious relationships with nature and nurture spiritual growth.

February 29 (Leap Year)

When meditating, the devotee should be fully attentive to the purpose of practice, disregarding physical and psychological conditions while directing attention to contemplation of higher realities. Mental and sensory impulses should be restrained; desire for any experience but for that which contributes to authentic spiritual growth should be absent.

Affirmation

I am always awake to the truth of my being. Conscious of my permanent relationship with God, I pray wisely, meditate deeply, and live proficiently.

Abide in Your Real Nature

To be soul-centered and God-conscious, devote a few minutes each day to practice the following routine.

1. Sit quietly. Acknowledge your spiritual beingness. You are not the body, mind, or personality; you are an expressive aspect of God's consciousness. Do not try to become that which you already are; nurture awareness of the reality of your being until you vividly experience it. Sit for as long as necessary until a shift of viewpoint occurs. If you sit patiently, waiting and watching, it will happen. The reality of God is always around you and through you, and is individualized as you.

2. Rest in clear awareness of wholeness until all thoughts and moods cease to be influential.

3. Poised in conscious awareness of your true nature, conclude the practice session. Remain peaceful, emotionally calm, and alert. Discern the difference between your true Self as a changeless being of pure consciousness and your thoughts and moods. Dispassionately observe circumstances and events. Perform all actions with conscious intention while being receptive to unplanned good fortune Know that God's grace always flows to support and provide for you.

My constant awareness of the presence of God is my assurance of continuing, permanent fulfillment.

MARCH

March 1

Even if we do not have a clear idea of what God is when we start on the spiritual path, when we sincerely endeavor to live righteously and engage in spiritual practices, the presence of God can be experienced.

March 2

To be healthy, happy, and in the flow of good fortune, we need to be spiritually awake and in harmonious accord with the rhythms of life. Passive, confused, wishful thinking, or erratic behaviors, will not produce the results we desire and deserve.

March 3

To accomplish meaningful purposes it is necessary to have a clearly defined vision of possibilities for their accomplishment. It is then easier to choose thoughts, emotional states, relationships, and actions which support effective living and spiritual growth.

Seek first to know and experience the reality of God,
and live righteously, and all these things [whatever is needed
for well-being] will be provided.
— *New Testament / Matthew 6:33* —

March 4

Writing our clearly defined purposes confirms our decision to accomplish them and attunes our awareness and mental processes with Universal Mind. Firm resolve, conviction, and concentrated intention empowers us to think and act effectively and our attunement with Universal Mind attracts a supportive response.

March 5

When the intellectual faculty is purified, superior powers of discernment can be demonstrated. When intuition is unfettered, the truth about whatever is examined can be known. When awareness of our true nature is unobscured, we are enlightened.

March 6

Absolute liberation of consciousness is the ideal of the spiritual aspirant whose commitment to the spiritual path is total. Individuals with weak or inconstant resolve tend to compromise: to be satisfied with limited freedom which affords them only a degree of temporary comfort. Resolve to be awake in God.

Few people know that the wholeness
of God extends fully to this Earth realm.
— *Mahavatar Babaji, guru of Lahiri Mahasaya* —

March 7

Pessimists cause their own unhappiness and tend to nurture thoughts and feelings of sadness and despair. Optimists choose to see the good and the possible and are always happy, enthusiastic, and energetic.

March 8

Because the reality of God is always fully present where we are, we can be Self-realized, healthy, affluent, freely expressive, and fulfilled in this world.

March 9

This world is our temporary abode. Our true origin is inner space, the transcendent field of unmodified Consciousness-Existence from which we emerged into the realm of nature and to which we are destined to return. While we are embodied, the reality of God can be known by prayer and contemplative meditation. We can also instantaneously awaken to realization of God.

Read a little; meditate more; think of God always.
— *Paramahansa Yogananda* —

March 10

When the mind and body have been sufficiently prepared, advanced meditation processes can be practiced to quicken the spiritual growth process. The actions of inward grace also produce beneficial effects.

March 11

The key to effective meditation is to practice with alert attention. Short meditation sessions elicit relaxation and mental calm, provide physical and psychological benefits, and contribute to gradual spiritual growth. Longer, deeper practice subdues mental processes, allowing superconscious perceptions. In the deep silence, merge your awareness in God.

March 12

When meditating, physical sensations, thoughts, moods, and memories should be ignored. Aspire to awaken to levels of awareness which are not dependent upon objects of perception—thoughts, mental visions, feelings of various kinds however pleasant. Be satisfied only with realization of wholeness.

If you continue to do as I have taught you, then you are
my disciples indeed; and you shall know the truth, and
the truth shall make you free.
— *The Gospel According to Saint John 8:31,32* —

March 13

There will never be a better time than now to be committed to right living and spiritual growth. We are immortal beings destined to awaken in God. If we sincerely want to, we can be Self-realized in this incarnation. We can completely awaken from the dream of mortality and be fully liberated.

March 14

Listen to and heed the wise counsel of enlightened people. Be inspired by the example of their lives and be Self-motivated to your highest good. Remember, however, that we must know the truth for ourselves and have it actualized in our lives. The Self-realization that others have cannot liberate our consciousness. Only our Self-realization frees us from unknowing.

Self-realization can be accomplished quickly by surrendering in God. God [the Oversoul] with attributes, arises from the field of Supreme [Absolute] Consciousness. [In relationship to Nature] God is transcendent and endowed with omniscience, omnipotence, and omnipresence. That Supreme Being, beyond the boundaries of space, time, and causation, is the true guru [teacher] of even the ancient teachers.
— *Patanjali's yoga-sutras 1:24–26* —

March 15

Because the fullness of the reality of God is present where we are, and we are flawless expressions of God's consciousness, we can experience personal fulfillment and spiritual illumination here and now. Be established in spiritual awareness and live accordingly.

March 16

Affirmation: "I acknowledge that the full reality of God is present and expressive where I am. My clear and constant awareness of the reality of the Presence of God is the basis of my complete fulfillment."

March 17

Inspiration is a divine influence upon the mind and emotions that awakens imagination and incites us to idealistic thinking and constructive actions. Inspiration infuses the mind and body with the soul's spiritual forces, awakens intuition, and causes us to desire excellence in actions, relationships, and circumstances.

I am truly that Supreme Consciousness, which is eternal, stainless and free, one, indivisible, nondual, and which is bliss, truth, knowledge, and infinite.
— *Adi Shankara* —

March 18

Inspiration removes dullness, confusion, and pessimism from the mind and provides a glimpse of transcendent realities. Nurture inspiration with optimism, prayer, meditation, and attentive practice of the presence of God.

March 19

Remind yourself that, as a spiritual being, you are meant to be healthy-minded, problem-free, happy, functionally effective, prosperous, and successful. If you believe otherwise, it is only because habits of negative thinking have been allowed to be influential. Use your powers of intelligence. Be a rational, positive thinker.

March 20

Don't be so obsessed with formal practice of spiritual exercises that you neglect mundane duties and responsibilities, nor be so compulsive about satisfying desires and accomplishing personal purposes that remembrance of God is neglected. A life lived without awareness of God is superficial and unsatisfying.

That state which ever *is*, is available to all
with perfect, natural ease.
— *Sri Ramana Maharishi* —

March 21

Whatever you can vividly imagine, ardently believe, and comfortably accept as being possible for you to have or experience, can be manifested in your life. Through your mind, you interact with Universal Mind which produces or makes possible what you habitually think about and are receptive to having and experiencing.

March 22

Outgrow the idea that God is a cosmic parent-figure, that you are separate from God, and all other limiting beliefs. Learn to perceive accurately to avoid illusions which cloud awareness and interfere with rational thinking. Be willing to grow to emotional maturity: to be responsible for your well-being, choices, and actions. Be anchored in God-realization.

You are told that you should love your neighbor as yourself; but if you love yourself meanly, childishly, timidly, even so shall you love your neighbor. Learn to love yourself with a love that is wise and healthy, that is large and complete.
— *Maurice Maeterlinck / Wisdom and Destiny* —

March 23

Discard thoughts, behaviors, relationships, and actions which are inconsistent with your highest ideals. Whatever concept of the ideal life you have, actualize it now. You do not have to wait to make useful changes.

March 24

Once resolved on a constructive course of action, persist on your chosen course until the desired results are manifested. Be soul-centered. Go deeper into God while faithfully continuing to do what is useful.

March 25

God's grace expresses as the supportive, enlivening influence that contributes to planetary transformation and to our personal and spiritual fulfillment. Grace flows freely and expresses in our field of awareness to harmonize physical functions, organize mental processes, and awaken soul capacities and qualities. It expresses around us to unfold supportive events, relationships, and circumstances. Its actions are effortless and always result in the highest good.

In returning and rest shall you be saved;
in quietness and in confidence shall be your strength.
— *The Book of the Prophet Isaiah 30:15* —

March 26

When we are Self-realized, our inner light radiates to others and to the world, our mental peace is a calming influence, and our orderly behaviors demonstrate our purposefulness. The truth-consciousness that we share with others is of God.

March 27

We do not have to approve of the misbehavior of others or allow ourselves to be hurt or inconvenienced by it. We can see through behaviors and personality characteristics to the inner, divine essence of every person. Learn to see that innate divinity.

March 28

Generous, appropriate giving prospers us because it enables us to remain aware of the wholeness of life. This kind of giving is not wasteful, nor is it done with a self-limiting, bargaining mental attitude. See needs and fill them. See hurts and heal them.

The things that we see about us are God's thoughts
and words to us; and if we were but wise there is not a
step that we take which we should not find to be full
of mighty instruction.
— *Charles Haddon Spurgeon / Sermons* —

March 29

To think in terms of giving to receive puts limits on what can unfold in our daily experience. The constructive attitude to have is to know that, as we are open to life, life spontaneously provides whatever is needed. Renounce thoughts of limitation. Cultivate an awareness of freedom and abundance. Be in the flow.

March 30

Do not withhold your good will and kind thoughts. Be thankful when you learn of the good fortune of others. God's blessings flow equally to everyone.

March 31

To be a renunciate is to be in harmonious accord with others and with circumstances without mental or emotional attachments. The key to renunciation is to be soul-centered, without dependence upon externals. Nothing of real value is forsaken by Self-realized renunciation. Abide in the Source of everything.

Affirmation

Attuned to Infinite Consciousness, whatever I clearly
envision and truly believe, I flawlessly demonstrate
and experience in daily life.

Write Your Hopes, Dreams, and Plans for
Fulfilling All of Your Meaningful Purposes

For your life to be meaningful, have clearly defined purposes. You need not know exactly how they will be fulfilled when you first write your hopes and dreams. Think about your future and visualize what you want to experience and accomplish. Meditate quietly until you sense the presence of God, then clearly and concisely write from the innermost level of your being.

*living in love
and always Being
Love*

To help to make possible the fulfillment of all of my meaningful purposes I will:

*Read and write
as often as I can
and connect with
other Beings as much as
possible*

I see clearly now; I rejoice in understanding.

APRIL

April 1

There are many helpful things we can do to remove our awareness from the restless mind and surging senses. The final freedom is due to God's grace.

April 2

God's grace expresses from within us because there is no separation between the soul and God; it expresses around us because God is all-pervading. God's grace causes our spontaneous spiritual unfoldments, the unplanned and unanticipated supportive events and circumstances we frequently experience, and the final removal of delusion (unknowing) from our awareness.

April 3

The highest knowledge is that which enables us to comprehend the truth about life and to observe all circumstances with equanimity. Thus permanently established in Self-realization, our highest good is unfolded and there is nothing more to which to aspire.

If I honor my myself, my honor is nothing.
— *The Gospel According to Saint John 8:54* —

April 4

Our progress in spiritual growth can be accurately determined by self-observation of our mental and emotional states and functional behaviors. If we are always mentally calm, emotionally stable, cheerfully willing to be responsible for our thoughts, moods, and behaviors, and are able to attend to duties and accomplish purposes skillfully and efficiently, our soul qualities are being effectively demonstrated or actualized.

April 5

In the midst of our chosen or obligatory duties and activities, we may sometimes forget that our most important duty is to always be awake in God. Only when our soul qualities are unfolded and actualized can we be healthy-minded, creatively functional, and spiritually capable of being of real value to society.

April 6

Affirm: "When my attention is distracted and my awareness of the presence of God begins to diminish, I rest in the sanctuary of the soul until my mind is refreshed and my consciousness is illumined."

Like a drop of water from the sea and a grain of sand,
so are a few years in the day of eternity.
— *The Old Testament Apocrypha / Ecclesiasticus 18:10* —

April 7

Millions of souls in this world and in other realms are not yet aware of the potential they have to know realities beyond the mind and senses. If you intuitively glimpse what is possible for you to ultimately know and experience, now is the time to desire with all of the concentrated endeavor of your being the complete unfoldment of your innate capacities and qualities.

April 8

A disciple* is capable of acquiring knowledge and applying it to moral, mental, and spiritual development. By learning and self-training, a dedicated disciple regulates thoughts, emotions, sensory impulses, and behaviors with conscious intention to accomplish purposes which are known to be worthwhile.

* Latin *discipulus*, pupil, from *descere*, to learn.

God is the ocean of Spirit; human beings are like waves that rise and fall on the ocean's surface. To one who is involved in the drama of relative life—who is attached to success and fearful of failure; attached to good health and fearful of illness; attached to material existence and fearful of death— the endlessly varied human experiences appear to be the only reality. To one who is perfectly established in nonattachment, everything is perceived as God.
— *Paramahansa Yogananda* —

April 9

Some causes of resistance to learning new ideas and behaviors are egotism, complacency, uncertainty, mental perversity, fear of the unknown, fear of failure, and strong attachment to present circumstances.

April 10

Egotism, an **excessive** sense of self-importance often dramatized as arrogance, is grounded in ignorance of the true nature of the soul in relationship to God and nurtured by feelings of insecurity. When Self-knowledge dawns, egotism is replaced by humility.

April 11

To be complacent is to settle for limited understanding and restricting circumstances rather than to learn their causes and overcome or transcend them. A devotee of God will not compromise; only complete unfoldment of innate knowledge and circumstances that reflect the highest good will satisfy the soul.

Whoever, either now or after I am gone, shall be a lamp unto themselves and a refuge unto themselves, shall not seek an external refuge, but holding fast to the truth as their lamp ... it is they who shall attain the topmost height. But they must be intent on learning.
— *Words attributed to Gautama Buddha* —

April 12

Avoid endeavors to create a strong, artificial sense of personality-based self-esteem. It is more useful, and psychologically transformative, to be Self-confident because grounded in awareness and knowledge of ourselves as individualized units of God's consciousness.

April 13

Overcome fear by learning to enjoy the adventure of discovery. Armed with knowledge of the principles of causes and their effects, know that right endeavor supported by firm resolve will definitely produce worthwhile results. Claim the good fortune you deserve.

April 14

Affirmation: "Whenever my interest in relationships of any kind becomes obsessive and I begin to lose my objectivity, I look to the Source of everything, knowing it to be my primary relationship."

The finite mind generates countless ideas within itself which weaken it and veil perception of truth. These cause impressions and tendencies in the mind which are, for the most part, latent or dormant. When the mind is rid of them, the veil vanishes in a moment like mist at sunrise, and with it the greatest sorrows also vanish.
— *Ancient yoga text* —

April 15

Train yourself to be Self-motivated: to be inspired from the depths of your being rather than rely on your random thoughts, changing moods, or to be dependent on the encouragement of others. The same intelligence and power that illumines the minds of saints and flows through them to accomplish constructive purposes, is within you. Learn to let the power of God flow through you.

April 16

Compulsive habits of personal behavior and indiscriminate choices of mundane experiences and relationships confine our awareness and restrict spiritual growth. To restore soul awareness to wholeness, live wisely and effectively with conscious intention.

April 17

All endeavors to attempt to create an enduring monument to ourselves in this world are misdirected and doomed to failure. Be anchored in God, letting the results of your wisely performed, constructive actions be your selfless service to the universe.

You are on Earth for but a little while, and your real reason for being here is very different from what you may have imagined. If you want God's guidance in your life, don't waste time in idle talk with others. Silence is the altar of Spirit.
— *Paramahansa Yogananda* —

April 18

In the darkest of our dark nights, the inner light ever shines. To know that God is the reality of our lives is to be imbued with hope, to have faith that, regardless of any condition which may challenge us, our highest good is assured. The Intelligence-Power that produced the worlds is superior to any situation.

April 19

Train yourself to be absolutely fearless in the face of trouble of any kind. Circumstances are only appearances on the screen of space-time. Their supporting causes can be modified or removed by right understanding and skillful actions. Life's processes are ever-becoming, always flowing and changing.

April 20

Prophets of doom are intellectually incompetent and emotionally disturbed. They are either unaware of or are not capable of comprehending the God-impelled processes of evolution that are transforming nature and assisting the spiritual awakening of souls.

Courage, my mind; God is our helper. God made us, and not we ourselves. Press on where the truth begins to dawn.
— *Saint Augustine* —

April 21

We cannot permanently hide from God because we cannot forever ignore our own divinity. While we play with our thoughts and feelings and endeavor to cling to our fragile sense of independent selfhood, at a deeper level our soul awareness remains ever free and blissful. Acknowledge your true Self. Let it emerge.

April 22

Superconsciousness is the natural state of the soul. When the soul is partially awake, superconscious states are modified by thoughts and emotional states. When the soul is fully awake, restricting influences are permanently transcended. Be awake to your true Self.

April 23

Superconsciousness differs from ordinary waking states during which awareness is fragmented by mental fluctuations and transformations, and from subconscious and unconscious states. When thoughts are stilled, superconsciousness emerges.

To define yourself in terms of human limitations
is a desecration of the image of God you are.
— *Paramahansa Yogananda* —

April 24

When, during meditation or at other times, refined superconscious states are experienced, the soul's innate knowledge is spontaneously unfolded. The reality of life's wholeness is then effortlessly apprehended.

April 25

Ask, and it will be provided for you. When calm, and clear in your mind about what is best for you, don't be afraid or ashamed to ask the universe to provide for your needs. Decide how your life should be experienced and invite the universe to be supportive of you.

April 26

Seek, and you will surely discover. Be a possibility-thinker. After an interlude of tranquil meditation, open your mind to "what can be so" for you. Think of ways to help yourself to fulfillment of life-enhancing purposes. Insights will surface in your awareness. Innovative ideas will flow. Opportunities will be presented to you.

Except the Lord build the house, they labor in vain
who build it; except the Lord keep the city, the
watchman awakens but in vain.
— *The Book of Psalms 127:1* —

April 27

Persistently inquire, and you will be Self-realized. Daily contemplate the truth of your innermost level of being and the reality of God. You have the capacity to be fully awake in God and to live joyously in tune with the Infinite. Don't dwell on memories of past events. Refuse to be distracted. Be spiritually conscious.

April 28

Your choices and actions of the moment determine your near and distant future experiences. Choose wisely and act decisively. Your highest good is available to you.

April 29

The perfecting results of patience are experienced when we are established in soul awareness and intent upon discovering the truth about God and ourselves. The redemptive outcome of our focused endeavor is realization of our innate perfection.

To understand what our natural needs are, we should rely on observation, experimentation, and reason.
— *Sri Yukteswar* —

April 30

When we did not know the truth about ourselves we were inclined to make mistakes. Now that we know that we are spiritual beings abiding in God, the situation is different; we can no longer pretend to be unaware of our relationship with the Infinite. We can no longer ignore our duty to be responsible for wise and constructive use of our knowledge, abilities, and resources.

Affirmation

Established in soul contentment, ever inspired, always aspiring to the highest good, sustaining clear perceptions of possibilities, attentive to acquiring knowledge, intentional in right endeavors, firm in faith, and persisting on the path in life I know to be best for me, I am ever receptive and responsive to the actions of the life-enhancing, freely expressive grace of God.

Your Spiritual Practice Routines

The basis of total wellness and fulfillment of life's purposes is commitment to a program of learning to acquire knowledge that will enable you to live effectively and to regularly engage in practices which can facilitate your spiritual growth. Write your program for learning and spiritual practice and implement it immediately. If you are already a committed devotee of God, review your studies and practices and make improvements if necessary.

1. My secular and philosophical learning program is:

_____

_____

_____

2. My daily prayer and meditation routine is:

_____

_____

_____

_____

I pray, meditate, and live in God.

MAY

May 1

Ask these questions and let your soul response reveal the answers. What is evolution endeavoring to accomplish? How can I participate with evolutionary processes to fulfill my purposes? How can I live more effectively and be of benefit to others?

May 2

Unenlightened behaviors serve only the egocentric self. The wiser way to live is to aspire to spiritual growth and to unfold and express soul qualities. The more we heed the soul's inclination to be unconfined and knowledgeably expressive, the greater is our happiness. Think rationally. Use your powers of intuition.

May 3

The mind is constantly being impressed by thoughts and sensory perceptions. Let it also be influenced by meditative superconscious realizations.

Keeping on, keeping on; one day, behold! the divine goal.
— *Lahiri Mahasaya* —

May 4

After meditation, continue to sit calmly for a few minutes. Let your soul radiance illumine your mind and infuse your body. Know and feel yourself to be in harmony with the rhythms of life. Acknowledge all souls and wish for them their total well-being and spiritual fulfillment. Rest in the silence until you are firmly established in realization of wholeness.

May 5

When obstacles to subjective perception are removed, we become aware of the reality of God that pervades the universe. It was not apprehended before because our attention was too involved with the self-conscious condition and with illusional ideas.

May 6

Spontaneous subjective insights often pleasantly surprise us. Remain alert and attentive, prepared for those moments of insightful discovery.

The soul, when it has driven away from itself all
that is contrary to the Divine Will, becomes transformed
in God in Love. It then becomes immediately enlightened
by and transformed in God.
— *St. John of the Cross* —

May 7

Affirm: "I know the natural way to live which nurtures total my well-being and spiritual growth. For my highest good, ever soul-directed and insightfully purposeful, I attentively adhere to this natural way."

May 8

Nothing external to ourselves blesses or deprives us. Our own states of consciousness, mental states, and habitual behaviors determine our experiences. When we learn how to live effectively and choose to do so, we experience continuous good fortune and spiritual fulfillment.

May 9

Discipleship is easy for the surrendered devotee; it is difficult for the unsurrendered. Four troublesome habits to overcome on the discipleship path are anger, resentment, self-centered willfulness, and self-pity.

Better than rulership over all the worlds, better than going to heaven, is the reward of the first step in holiness.
— *The Dhammapada ("Words of the Doctrine")* —

May 10

We do not have to be cloistered to grow spiritually. So long as our lifestyle is wholesome, duties are attentively fulfilled, and actions are performed without mental or emotional attachment to them or to their results, soul unfoldment can proceed smoothly.

May 11

Four prerequisites for success on the discipleship path are sufficient intelligence to comprehend what is to be learned, renunciation of invalid opinions and addictive and self-defeating behaviors, ethical living, and sustained aspiration to be liberated.

May 12

Learning, reflection, and meditation are but three discipleship practices to be applied. What is learned should be intellectually and intuitively contemplated until it is fully comprehended. For authentic spiritual growth, superconscious meditation should be faithfully and correctly practiced.

One may know the world without going out of doors. One may see the Way of Heaven without looking through the windows. The further one goes, the less one knows. Therefore, the sage knows without going about, understands without seeing, and accomplishes without action.
— *Lao-tsu* —

May 13

It is easy to know what we consider to be of greater value. What do we think about most of the time? What do we desire above all else? To what do we primarily direct our attention, energies, talents, and resources?

May 14

Only peace can satisfy the restless mind. Only realization of God can satisfy the soul's yearning for fulfillment. Choose to be peaceful and God-realized.

May 15

Whatever you think or can imagine God to be, that idea can be the beginning of your relationship with God. As your understanding improves, you will discover that God is not at all what you first thought or imagined.

When the waves of consciousness are transcended by concentrated meditation practice, consciousness, being purified, experiences oneness with the Supreme Self. The manifested world, the [truth] seeker's consciousness, and Supreme Consciousness are experienced as one.
— *Lahiri Mahasaya* —

May 16

What originated your involvement with the realm of nature and has sustained and provided for you? What will be the conclusion of the drama of life you are now experiencing? The reality of God indwelling you will ensure your well-being and progressive spiritual awakening. Trust it. Be responsive to it.

May 17

When we say it is human nature to behave in certain ways, we are acknowledging that acquired or instinctive modes of behavior are often characteristic of us and of others whom we know. While observing the human condition, we can also be aware of our divine nature. We can live with Self-determined intention rather than as creatures of habit or circumstances.

May 18

It is of obvious benefit to us to be able to overcome misfortune such as illness, accidental injury, personality conflicts, financial difficulty, job loss, or other troublesome circumstances. After a personal problem is solved, we should endeavor to live skillfully so that life-inhibiting difficulties are avoided in the future.

That person is wisest who aspires to know God.
That person is most successful who realizes God.
— *Paramahansa Yogananda* —

May 19

Some common causes of personal misfortune are lack of knowledge of how to think and act constructively, habitual thinking and behavior that attracts misfortune, willful behavior even though we know better, disordered or undisciplined thinking, inattentiveness, and the habit of erroneously believing that difficulties of various kinds are normal conditions.

May 20

When having difficulty relating to another person, try to improve your communication with that person while remaining calm and radiating good will.

May 21

At all times, maintain your soul awareness and think and act rationally. You can entirely avoid conflict and misfortune by being firmly established in knowing that it is no longer possible for you to experience any condition that is not harmonious and constructive.

Pray like this: "God, I will reason, I will will, I will act;
please guide my reason, will, and activity so that I do
what you would have me do."
— *Paramahansa Yogananda* —

May 22

The primary cause of problems is insufficient spiritual awareness and understanding. When awareness and knowledge of our true nature is lacking, we may think of ourselves as mere human creatures. The final solution to all problems is spiritual awakening that removes our awareness from all illusions.

May 23

Affirm: "I discern the difference between myself as the observer and that which I observe. Thus ever discerning, I live comfortably and gracefully in the world with flawless understanding."

May 24

That which exists is real or actual. A circumstance or event is an actualization of its cause. Whether we are aware of it or not, our habitual mental states and actions are always causing our desires to manifest.

There is nothing to test the perfection of love better than trust. Wholehearted love ... carries confidence with it. Whatever one dares to trust God for, is found in God and a thousand times more.
— *Meister Eckhart* —

May 25

Even though we endeavor to perform actions to cause desired effects to be actualized, if we harbor thoughts and expectations to the contrary, we may attract corresponding circumstances or unconsciously perform actions which defeat our purposes. Live with conscious intention.

May 26

Why do some people remain attached to conflicted psychological states and distorted perceptions of themselves and their environment? They do so because they are in bondage to their unconscious or consciously self-chosen ignorance of the truth about themselves.

May 27

When clear realization of our spiritual reality is constant, our enlightenment is naturally and spontaneously expressed in every aspect of our lives.

From whence has this weakness come to you at this difficult time? It does not lead to spiritual fulfillment. Yield not to this immature behavior ... abandon this dramatization of weakness and faintheartedness. Be courageous!
— *Bhagavad Gita 2:2,3* —

May 28

To make your spiritual growth easier, cultivate awareness of the presence of God, live in accord with your highest understanding, and meditate long and deep in the silence. Be always anchored in the Infinite.

May 29

In meditative silence, rest in knowledge and awareness of yourself as a spiritual being. Sit for as long as necessary until an adjustment of awareness occurs that enables you to experience this truth about yourself.

May 30

Rest in meditative silence until all thoughts and feelings are quieted and you are alone in God. Poised in Self-realization, return your attention to your thoughts and perceptions of objective circumstances. Now soul-centered, make wise choices and implement appropriate actions as necessary. Know that God's grace ever flows to nurture and support you.

At the spiritual eye, the light of God shines.
The spiritual eye is the inner door that leads the soul's
awareness into the realm of the divine glory of God.
God dwells in each person and can be known when one
enters the sanctuary of pure, illumined consciousness.
— *Lahiri Mahasaya* —

May 31

The unillumined mind is clouded by beliefs, opinions, memories, desires, and various tendencies. Behind the clouds of the conditioned mind, the light of the soul remains undiminished. Three constituent characteristics of nature are influential in the mind: inertia contributes to mental dullness and blurs awareness; transformative influences incite the mind's actions and support its primary function of processing information; illuminating influences purify the mind and clear awareness. Choose thoughts, emotional states, behaviors, foods, and relationships which increase illuminating influences on the mind and body.

Affirmation

I live constructively with unwavering faith and appropriate, skillful actions. With cheerful resolve and unwavering trust in God I am steadfast on the spiritual awakening path.

Your Self-Transformation Practices

Although purposeful living and spiritual practices contribute to psychological health, it can also be helpful to be aware of mental attitudes and emotional states that need improvement. Remember that you are a spiritual being with freedom to choose your thoughts and emotions.

1. My mental attitudes and emotional states that need to be changed or improved:

_____

_____

2. To effect necessary changes or improvements I will:

_____

_____

3. My behaviors that need to be changed or improved:

_____

4. To change or improve my behaviors I will:

_____

_____

My mind is well-ordered, I am emotionally stable;
I am spiritually renewed.

JUNE

June 1

There is an obvious difference between passive sympathy and active compassion. We may sympathize with someone and identify with their discomfort, yet do nothing to attempt to alleviate it. We demonstrate true compassion when we are capable of helping someone who is in trouble, and willingly and effectively do it.

June 2

Compassionate behavior is moral behavior. It is always supportive, never harmful. Moral thoughts and behaviors contribute to harmony and well-being; immoral thoughts and behaviors contribute to disorder.

June 3

Morality is the basis of right living because ideal personal conduct is supportive of us, society, and nature. It keeps us in harmonious relationship with the universe and sustains our attunement with the Infinite.

Agape is a unique type of love, a love that pours
itself out regardless of merit ... it floods out like the
sun to reach the just and the unjust.
— *Rufus Jones / Pathways to the Reality of God* —

June 4

Until we are fully enlightened, effective living facilitates cooperative personal relationships, and the removal of mental and physical restrictions to spiritual growth. As our soul qualities unfold and become influential, we are naturally inclined to think and behave constructively. Right living is then effortless and enjoyable because soul-inspired and impelled.

June 5

We cannot have meaningful relationships with others until we are at peace within ourselves. Peace of soul is realized when we consciously abide in God.

June 6

Self-knowledge reveals to us that all living beings are expressive units of God's consciousness. We are then naturally inclined to care about the welfare of all souls and to want to assist them to their highest good.

Use me, God, in your great harvest field, which stretches far and wide like a wide sea. The gatherers are few; I fear the precious yield will suffer loss. Oh, find a place for me!
— *Christina Rosetti (19th century)* —

June 7

Do you know someone who could benefit from your compassionate actions? What can you do to be helpful? While charitable (loving) thoughts and prayers are always supportive, appropriate actions are often needed. Think about the real needs of people whom you know, and do what you can to assist them to learn about, awaken to, and actualize their innate potential.

June 8

Examine your thoughts and feelings. Do you sometimes think about limitations and feel confined and frustrated, or is it easy for you to think and know that, with God, your highest good is always possible? Your thoughts and feelings reflect your habitual states of consciousness and personal choices. Be established in Self-realization. Rejoice in freedom.

June 9

As souls, we are like bubbles in the infinite ocean of God's consciousness. We are always in God and we share a common sameness with all souls.

... faith is the substance of things hoped
for, the evidence of things unseen.
— *New Testament / Hebrews 11:1* —

June 10

If we listen carefully, we can hear the universe speaking to us: "What do you want?" it asks. Then it confides, "If you will but choose it, I will surely give it to you." What do you want more than anything else?

June 11

Affirm: "I choose to be consciously, spiritually awake. I choose to have harmonious relationships. I choose to thrive, flourish, and be successful in every way. I choose to fulfill my spiritual destiny. Fully committed to my soul-inspired choices, I always do everything necessary to allow them to be actualized!

June 12

Meditation is the process of withdrawing attention from the senses and from mental activities while directing it inward to the essence of our being and to God. The essence of our being is Self-sufficient pure consciousness which requires no external support. Our true Self is individualized God consciousness.

God is without beginning or end, complete,
and eternal; the one, indivisible being.
— *Sri Yukteswar* —

June 13

Schedule private time every day to be alone in God. Sit upright, relaxed and alert. Pray to invoke awareness of God's presence. If meditation flows spontaneously, directed by your innate impulse to have awareness restored to wholeness, rest in the silence and let super-conscious states unfold. Remain attentive to the process. Surrender self-consciousness. Let your sense of personal selfhood dissolve as awareness of your true Self as pure consciousness is revealed to you.

June 14

If meditation does not proceed spontaneously, use a meditation technique to elicit physical relaxation, quiet the mind, and improve concentration. Observe the natural flow of breathing, mentally listen to your chosen word, word-phrase or mantra, or use any procedure you know to be helpful. Practice of a meditation technique is a preliminary procedure. When the mind is quiet, patiently sit in the silence. Don't try to cause anything to happen. Be still, watching and waiting.

Meditation is the conscious awareness of the presence of God within us. It is the constant remembrance of the transcendental Spirit within our consciousness. God is revealed within us when our consciousness is made pure by liberating it from all concepts of duality and finitude.
— *Lahiri Mahasaya* —

June 15

The word "God" comforts the mind and satisfies the soul. In the early stages of meditation, be aware of your breathing rhythm. Mentally recite the word "God" when you inhale and when you exhale. When your attention is internalized, mentally listen to the word without reciting it. When the mental sound of the word is very subtle, discard it and flow into the silence.

June 16

An attractive word-phrase is "Om-God." Listen to the word "Om" with inhalation and to the word "God" when exhaling. Do this until relaxed and mentally calm. Meditation will then occur spontaneously.

June 17

Listen within to discern subtle sounds that arise in your field of awareness. Whatever sound you hear, gently endeavor to hear a more subtle sound behind it. Continue until the subtlest sound you hear is constant, and use it as your meditation mantra.

The practitioner of yoga should steadfastly contemplate the Supreme Reality, remaining in solitude, alone, with mind and body controlled, having no cravings for anything.
— *Bhagavad Gita 6:10* —

June 18

Presume the subtle, constant inner sound that you hear to be an aspect of the Word, the Om vibration pervading the universe. Merge in it. Expand your awareness in it. To experience pure consciousness, your essential nature, follow the sound to its source.

June 19

If you have been taught other helpful meditation techniques by a knowledgeable teacher, use them with benefit, remembering that they are like tools to be used to accomplish a specific purpose. Use them skillfully and effectively, then put them aside.

June 20

If you perceive light in the spiritual eye center, let your attention be attracted to it. When the mind is calm, clear white light may be perceived. Perceptions of forms and other visual phenomena are produced by the mind and brain. Ignore them.

Established in a comfortable, steady meditation
posture, in a clean, appropriate place; there, intent upon
practice, with thoughts and senses controlled, the yogi
should meditate to purify the mind.
— *Bhagavad Gita 6:11,12* —

June 21

When meditating, if it seems that nothing worthwhile is being experienced, relax. Sit patiently, watching and waiting with no preconceptions about the outcome. Remind yourself, "During my quiet time with God, there is nothing that is more important than what I am now doing." Learn to enjoy the soul's silence.

June 22

Whatever is perceived or felt when meditating is transitory. It is not your real Self. Avoid preoccupation with all perceptions of "otherness." Be satisfied only with Self-knowledge and God-realization.

June 23

In the silence, inquire, "What am I?" *Who* you think you are is your temporary sense of personal selfhood; *what* you are is an individualized expression of the consciousness of God. By attentive Self-inquiry, discover your true Self as changeless pure consciousness.

Holding the body, head, and neck erect, motionless and steady, gazing into the spiritual eye with focused attention; serene, fearless, established in self-control, with mental impulses subdued, concentrating on the Supreme Reality, the devotee should sit, devoted to the highest realization.
— *Bhagavad Gita 6:13,14* —

June 24

When mental transformations cease, the soul's pure consciousness is Self-revealed. By regular, attentive meditation practice, learn to be established in conscious realization of the truth of your being at all times.

June 25

Devotion without self-discipline can result in emotionalism, irrational thinking, and compulsive or misdirected actions. Balance devotional ardor with intellectual inquiry and commonsense behaviors.

June 26

Without awareness of ourselves as spiritual beings, our attempts to regulate mental and emotional states and behaviors will be only partially successful. Know that you are superior to your thoughts, moods, and actions.

Deep within us all there is an amazing inner sanctuary of the soul, a holy place, a Divine Center ... to which we may continuously return. Eternity is at our hearts, pressing upon our time-worn lives, warming us with intimations of an astounding destiny, calling us home to Itself.
— *Thomas R. Kelly / A Testament of Devotion* —

June 27

If possible, consecrate a private place to be used only for undisturbed interludes of prayer, meditation practice, and contemplative reflection. When you go there, disregard secular matters entirely. Think only of your relationship with God, then meditate deeply.

June 28

After meditating, established in the calmness elicited by attentive practice, live with intentional purpose. Meditation improves powers of concentration which enables you to make wise lifestyle choices. Intentional living improves functional skills which enables you to meditate more effectively.

June 29

Wholesome living, a well-ordered lifestyle, and progressive emergence of superconscious states experienced during repeated episodes of meditation practice purify the mind and refine the body to allow the soul's pure consciousness to be more efficiently expressed.

There is a spiritual sun that enlightens the soul more fully than the material sun. It as brilliant in the night as in the daytime; it is not without that it sheds its rays; it dwells within each of us.
— *François Fénelon / On the Existence of God* —

June 30

After fleeting episodes of Self-discovery, continue to meditate regularly to regenerate the body and to experience more profound, sustained transcendent realizations. Initial soul perceptions offer a promise of what is yet to unfold. Refuse to be satisfied with partial spiritual growth; be committed to completion of the process in this lifetime. Until innate knowledge is Self-revealed, you cannot know your personal history or how long you have been involved with material interests and your past actions and experiences. Take full advantage of the opportunity you now have to awaken completely in God. By right personal endeavor, and God's grace, you will surely succeed.

Affirmation

My resolve to know the full reality of God in this incarnation is definite and unwavering. Daily I abide in the sanctuary of the soul. In the deep silence, I am surrendered in God.

Your Regimens for Healthy, Long Life

Everything you do should be fully supportive of your meaningful purposes and your spiritual growth. Natural, wholesome living will confirm your noble resolves and allow them to more easily be actualized.

1. If you are in need of healing, what will you do to be restored to wholeness?

_____

_____

2. My routines for cleanliness, stress management, exercise, and other health practices are:

_____

_____

_____

3. A vegetarian diet is best. My choices of wholesome, nutritious food are:

_____

_____

The radiant, enlivening Spirit of God
is fully expressive through me.

JULY

July 1

Pray with devotion to become aware of the presence of God within and around you, then be still. Meditate quietly in that realization of wholeness. After meditating, if you feel led to pray for guidance, to have your needs met, or to accomplish purposes, pray for the welfare of others before you pray for yourself.

July 2

When praying for others, always selflessly pray for their highest good rather than for specific results. Do not endeavor to use will power to cause effects, or think that you know what is best for someone else. Avoid attempts to mentally manipulate or control others. Pray with a pure mind and a pure heart for the spiritual awakening and fulfillment of those for whom you pray. Have faith that your prayers are influential.

Therefore I say to you, whatever circumstances you
desire, when you pray, believe that you receive them,
and you shall have them.
— *New Testament / Mark 11:24* —

July 3

To pray for the well-being of all souls on Earth and in other realms, first meditate until your awareness is merged in God. Be established in the consciousness of wholeness. Listen to Om, the primordial sound pervading the universe. Apprehend omnipresence. Acknowledge God to be the reality of all souls.

July 4

When you pray for guidance, ask for it. It will emerge from within you as inspired ideas or be revealed to you through the words of others or as events and opportunities you encounter in daily life. Use your powers of intellectual discrimination to discern the difference between inspired ideas and wishful thinking, and to know whether to say yes or no to the many events, circumstances, and relationships that are made available to you. Be alert, think rationally, make wise choices.

There is a fundamental purpose for our lives. To recognize it
we must understand where life comes from and where it is
going. We must look beyond our immediate goals to what we
ultimately want to accomplish. We must consider life's
highest potential for development.
— *Paramahansa Yogananda* —

July 5

When praying to have needs met or to accomplish meaningful purposes, clearly define your needs and your projects in writing and keep a record of the results of prayer. Doing this will focus your thoughts and actions and increase your confidence in God and yourself.

July 6

God is the only Reality. God's being is individualized as souls. God's life enlivens the universe and living things. God's power expresses as energies, forces, and all of the manifestations of nature. There are no beings or powers apart from God. Otherness is nonexistent.

July 7

Just as universes are expressed from God's consciousness and manifested by God's Universal Mind, so our circumstances correspond to our states of consciousness and our mental states. Our circumstances are the result of our own choices and God's grace.

One should choose as a livelihood those activities which are consistent with *dharma* [that which upholds nature and society], adhere to the path of peace, and engage in studies to acquire useful knowledge. This is the way to happiness.
— *Charaka Samhita* / *An ancient text on Ayurveda* —

July 8

Flows of God's grace are inhibited when we choose to be self-centered, small-minded, irresponsible, or intellectually and physically lazy. Grace flows abundantly when we choose to be Self-aware, mentally expansive, responsible for our thoughts and actions, intellectually discerning, and engaged in constructive actions. Complete trust in God elicits the actions of grace.

July 9

Unwavering aspiration to be God-realized awakens dormant soul forces, clears the mind and awareness, and merges our consciousness with God's. When aspiration to be God-realized dominates our thoughts, it is easier to make wholesome lifestyle choices.

July 10

Master thoughts by cultivating optimism and by choosing to think constructively and rationally. Meditate to calm the mind and influence its actions to be more orderly. Associate with healthy-minded people. Identify with and emulate the behaviors of role models who are spiritually aware and functionally competent.

Great works do not always lie in our way, but every moment we may do little ones excellently, that is, with great love.
— *Saint Francis of Sales* —

July 11

Master states of consciousness by training yourself to go to sleep at will, awaken from sleep at a predetermined time, and immediately experience superconsciousness when you sit to meditate. Be Self-aware in the midst of activities and during interactions with others. Communicate effectively. Avoid excessive identification with thoughts, moods, and circumstances.

July 12

Master emotional states by soul-contentment, peace, and poise. Be even-minded. Maintain physical health. Don't allow memories of past misfortune or present perceptions of discord to disturb your soul peace. Avoid obsessive thinking, moodiness, and thoughts or feelings of despair. Live with meaningful purpose. Be happy. Be thankful for the opportunities you presently have to learn, creatively express, and actualize your spiritual potential.

Trust in God is greater than the magical power of the alchemist who creates treasures of gold by his art; for he alone who confides in God is independent and satisfied with what he has, and enjoys rest and peace without envying anyone else.
— *Bahya Ibn Paduka / The Duties of the Heart* —

July 13

Healthy, long life is of value because it allows us time and opportunity to acquire practical knowledge, fulfill obligations, accomplish purposes, and awaken to complete God-realization in the present life cycle. To be healthy, live in accord with nature's laws. To live long, have good reasons for doing so. While living realistically in this world remember that, at the soul level, you abide in eternity.

July 14

The most effective approach to total wellness is a life-management program with thoughtful attention given to spiritual, psychological, and physical health rather than to concentrate on one aspect and pay little heed to others. Be centered in spiritual awareness.

July 15

Never affirm ill health, poverty, limitations of any kind, or inability to be freely functional. God is equally present in and as all souls; remember this and think and act courageously. The power of God is innate to you.

From all blindness of heart, from pride, vainglory, and hypocrisy; from envy, hatred, and malice, and from all uncharitableness, Good Lord, deliver us.
— *The Book of Common Prayer* / *The Litany* —

July 16

So long as we identify with the limitations of the self-conscious state, they will tend to persist. What we presume to be true is what we are inclined to perceive and experience. What we direct our attention to is what we believe to be real. Discard all considerations of limitation and express your divine nature. You can.

July 17

So long as we affirm ourselves to be victims of our karma, inherited tendencies, planetary influences, or of any other external cause, until we decide otherwise, we will continue to experience the results of our misunderstanding. Awaken spiritually. Let innate knowledge of your invincibility unfold and prevail.

July 18

So long as we are satisfied to play the role of being a truth-seeker instead of a truth-knower, we will wander through space and time on a futile quest for truth—comprehension of the facts of life. That which we seek is not outside of us; it is within, at the very core of our being.

I never allow the word "impossible" to become
rooted in my mind; nor should you.
— *Paramahansa Yogananda* —

July 19

Religious rituals and spiritual practices performed without clear understanding and conscious intention cannot produce the results for which the soul yearns. Know why you do what you do. Act decisively. Quickly and definitely experience the results you desire.

July 20

The final knowledge that restores soul awareness to wholeness and liberates it, is Self-revealed in the illumined consciousness of all who succeed in awakening through the stages of spiritual growth by their focused endeavors and the redemptive actions of God's grace.

July 21

There are seven discernible stages through which souls awaken from ignorance of the truth about themselves to illumination of consciousness. To make spiritual growth easier, renounce behaviors and circumstances which restrict it, while cultivating behaviors and choosing circumstances which nurture it.

To be God-realized is to know your Self as the great ocean of Spirit by dissolving the delusion that you are this little ego, body, and personality.
— *Paramahansa Yogananda* —

July 22

Unconsciousness is characteristic of the first stage of the soul's involvement with matter, during which its awareness is so completely identified with the mind and the physical body that it mistakenly presumes itself to be a mind-body being. Some common symptoms are mental dullness, apathy, boredom, and provincialism. Rigid beliefs and unreasoned opinions tend to prevail. Spiritual awareness is minimal. Intellectual powers are weak and undeveloped. If one is religious, prayer is usually directed to one's mental concept of God. Belief in God and in ways to salvation is considered to be more important than knowledge. Spiritual fulfillment, if envisioned as a possibility, is usually thought of as being a future accomplishment. Activities are primarily survival-oriented, or as one is impelled by desires, whims, and peer-group influences. Memories, habits, learned or acquired behaviors, and social and cultural traditions tend to determine one's lifestyle. The soul's life forces are mostly dormant.

Self-realization is the knowing in all parts of your body, mind, and soul that you are wholly established in God. To be Self realized, you have only to improve your knowing.
— *Paramahansa Yogananda* —

July 23

Dysfunctional self-consciousness is characteristic of the second stage of soul awakening. Mental confusion along with irrational thinking and conflicted emotional states is common. Egocentric preoccupation with the illusional sense of personality-self prevails. One may be superstitious, fascinated with magic, endeavor to acquire supernatural powers, believe in angels, or be attracted to mediumship or "channeling" in misguided endeavors to communicate with beings in other spheres who are presumed to have exceptional knowledge. Powers of intellectual discrimination are weak. Addictions, sensual desires, compulsive cravings, obsessions, hallucinations, dependent emotional relationships, self-defeating behaviors, neurotic needs, complaints, faultfinding, and fantasies about everyday matters and higher realities are common. Emotions and subconscious conditionings tend to determine thinking and behavior. When meditating, one may be more interested in perceiving mental phenomena or having a religious experience than in spiritual growth. The soul's life forces are only partially aroused.

At fifteen, my mind was inclined toward learning; at thirty I stood firm; at forty, I was free from delusions; at fifty, I understood the will of God; at sixty, my ears were receptive to truth; at seventy, I could follow the promptings of my heart without overstepping the boundaries of right.
— *Confucius* —

July 24

Functional self-consciousness is characteristic of the third stage of soul awakening: a more superior, healthy-minded, yet still egocentric condition. Rational, nurturing choices usually determine behaviors and relationships. Goal-oriented actions are routinely performed with reasonable skill. Partial intellectual comprehension of the reality of God may be present, mixed with traditional or illusional beliefs. One may be more interested in accessing divine influences to acquire powers, improve functional skills, or control personal circumstances than in Self-discovery and God-realization. Meditation and prayer may be directed to physical and psychological improvement only, or used to enhance abilities for the purpose of accomplishing personal goals. While one may be curious about the metaphysical causes of mundane events and spiritual growth may be desired, interest in this-world projects and relationships tends to be more compelling. Characteristics common to the first two stages of soul unfoldment may also be present and influential. The soul's life forces are more awakened and soul consciousness is gradually emerging.

Somehow, somewhere, in the beginning, middle, or end
of our lives, or in all three, we are certain to meet with God.
— *Gamaliel Bradford* —

July 25

Superconsciousness is characteristic of the fourth level of soul awakening. Superconscious states emerge during meditative contemplation and are influential after meditation practice. The illusional sense of independent selfhood diminishes as Self-realization increases. Activities and relationships are wisely chosen and experienced without compulsion or attachments. Love of knowledge is intense. Willingness to live righteously and to engage in spiritual practices is apparent. Solitude is enjoyable. Renunciation of mental and emotional attachments is easier. Sensory and mental impulses are more easily regulated. Unwholesome thoughts, conversations, and lifestyle habits; unethical behaviors; and the company of ego-directed people are no longer appealing. Aspiration to liberation of consciousness is sincere and constant. One at this stage of soul unfoldment can be a competent disciple (learner) on the spiritual path. Some remaining characteristics common to the first three stages of soul awakening may interfere with endeavors to accomplish spiritual growth. These can be overcome by will power and choice or transcended as soul qualities become more expressive. The soul's life forces, now awakened, flow upward through the spinal pathway into the higher brain centers.

A well-regulated mind results in happiness.
— *The Dhammapada* / *Buddhist scripture* —

July 26

Cosmic conscious states are characteristic of the fifth level of soul awakening. As superconscious states become increasingly influential and self-consciousness diminishes, apprehension of the universe as an interaction of cosmic forces emanated from God's being improves. When meditating, perceptions and realizations are transcendent. The universe is comprehended as a manifestation of primordial nature: Om, and its self-expressions of space, time, and fine cosmic particles. Activities and relationships are enjoyed with higher understanding. Soul capacities expand to allow more vivid realization of the reality of God. Ignorance, selfishness, and indifference about the welfare of others cease as the soul qualities of knowledge, selflessness, and compassion become influential. Soul abilities become more pronounced and are wisely used. The soul's life forces flow without interference, removing restrictions to spiritual growth from the mind and transforming the physiology to enable it to process and sustain more refined, transcendent perceptions.

There are some souls who cannot dwell upon nor
engage their minds with any mystery; they are drawn
to a certain gentle simplicity before God, and held in
this simplicity, without other consideration save to
know that they are before God.
— *St. Francis of Sales* —

July 27

God-realization is characteristic of the sixth stage of soul awakening. If any mental conditionings yet remain, their influences are weakened and removed. Selfless, insightful actions prevent the accumulation of further mental conditionings. Meditation is easy, blissful, and spontaneous as determined by the soul's innate inclination to be fully awake in God and the impulses of grace. As God-realization increases, the soul awakens through successive stages of final awakening and experiences liberation of consciousness.

July 28

The final stage of soul awakening is complete enlightenment. When relating to mundane realms, the soul's enlightenment persists. All actions are spontaneously appropriate. God-realization is not restricted by the purified ego-sense which remains only as a viewpoint from which one dispassionately observes the universal drama.

Focus your attention within. You will experience new power, new strength, and new peace in body, mind, and spirit. When you do this, all bonds that limit you will be vanquished.
— *Paramahansa Yogananda* —

July 29

Spiritual growth is rapid when we diligently and wisely apply the valid knowledge that is acquired from authoritative sources and the Self-revealed knowledge that unfolds. The key to successful accomplishment of spiritual growth is to put knowledge to the test of experience; to prove it for ourselves.

July 30

To awaken to Self-knowledge and God-realization is the most unselfish act we can perform. When we are awake in God, the entire universe is beneficially influenced. The illuminating qualities of nature are strengthened, inertia is weakened, and the spiritual awakening of all souls in this and other realms is made easier. Our liberation assists others to liberation.

July 31

Time need not be a determining factor in relationship to spiritual growth. Many souls, having sojourned in the universe for thousands of years, are still unaware of their spiritual potential. Some are slowly, progressively awakening. Some are fully awake in God. You can quickly awaken if you aspire to do so.

Blessed are the pure in heart: for they shall see God.
— *New Testament* / *Matthew 5:8* —

Be Committed to Excellence

Skillful actions will keep you in harmonious accord with universal forces and their constructive processes. Be aware of your spiritual reality. Nurture functional skills and express them freely and creatively.

1. What latent abilities do you have that are yet to be unfolded? Learn to awaken and express them.

_____

_____

_____

2. What skills and are you constructively using?

_____

_____

3. What new skills are you interested in acquiring, and what will you do to acquire and proficiently use them?

_____

_____

_____

I use my abilities and skills wisely and constructively.

AUGUST

August 1

The knowledge innate to consciousness is the only reliable teacher. The thoughts and words of others can only inform us about truth; they are not truth itself.

August 2

The processes of spiritual growth are the result of consciousness referring to itself to unfold and express its innate potential. These processes can be enlivened and nurtured by sincere desire to be spiritually awake.

August 3

An enlightened soul, fully awake in God, can assist other souls to awaken. Their wise words can remind us of what we, at the innermost level of our being, already know. Their behaviors can indicate to us how we should live. When we are intuitively receptive, a glimpse of their God-realization can be wordlessly transmitted to us. A guru is a truth teacher-revealer.

There can be no substitute ... for the longing to be absolutely linked with the living God, with the Infinite Light.
— *Abraham Isaac Kook* —

August 4

A guru's primary function is to help souls discard the illusional consideration of personal selfhood: the erroneous notion of being other than a flawless, individualized expression of God's consciousness.

August 5

Many truth seekers, addicted to personal opinions and habits, err in thinking that the principles that determine spiritual growth change with the times or that social or cultural circumstances determine them.

August 6

Emotionally immature truth seekers may think that their desire to express their individuality and to assertively demonstrate self-determined independence requires a different relationship with a truth teacher: one that makes possible the apprehension of higher knowledge while allowing the preservation of the self-centered condition. Insightful analysis of this irrational idea reveals the obvious truth that ego-fixated awareness and illumination of consciousness cannot coexist.

If you see things in eternity, you are less a prey to the pain of their passing, so you can learn the more easily not to clutch at them as they pass.
— *Gerald Vann* —

August 7

Unlike invalid theories and passing fads that emerge, are popular for a brief duration of time, and dissolve into obscurity, the fundamental laws of consciousness are timeless. God remains ever the same. Souls are individualized expressions of God. Insufficient spiritual awareness is the primary cause of human suffering. Only authentic spiritual growth that culminates in Self-knowledge and God-realization can confer unwavering peace of mind and the permanent removal of delusions and illusions that cause suffering and misfortune.

August 8

Disciples (fully committed learners) on the spiritual path who are willing to renounce *egotism* (arrogance) and who allow *egoism* (self-consciousness) to diminish so that soul qualities can spontaneously unfold without interference, experience rapid progress. Disciples who are not yet committed to actualizing authentic spiritual growth are inclined to be inattentive and confused because of attachments to cherished opinions, existing circumstances, and ignorance of the truth. Affirm with conviction: "I choose to be alert, knowledgeable, and free."

I am not the guru. God is the guru; I am only God's servant.
— *Paramahansa Yogananda* —

August 9

How does one find a guru, a truth teacher-revealer? If one is destined to have a personal relationship with an enlightened teacher, it will happen. Until it does, one is advised to prepare for it by virtuous living and concentrated spiritual practice. Look to God, always.

August 10

Some souls prefer limitation to freedom because they have doubts about their ability to improve themselves or their circumstances. Ordinary, conditioned awareness is always subject to feelings of insecurity and inadequacy. When we are soul-centered, it is easy to have conviction and envision possibilities, and enjoyable to demonstrate our knowledge and skills.

August 11

If you are not yet enlightened, what will your life be like when you are fully awake to the truth of yourself and God? How will you think? What will you do? Think and act like an enlightened being now.

When your intelligence is firm in realization of oneness,
then shall you awaken to flawless Self-knowledge.
— *Bhagavad Gita 2:53* —

August 12

If God could speak in words we might hear: "I am the unchanging Self of all that is; I am the universe; I am all beings; I am you. Though I express in diverse ways, I am undivided, am not in the least influenced by events occurring in my Self-manifested realms, and am forever the impartial witness of all that occurs."

August 13

God does "speak" to us—not in the language of the mind but in the language of the heart—as impulses arising from the core of our innermost being that incline us to Self-discovery and spiritual growth.

August 14

Our affirmative response to the opportunity we have to choose to be Self-realized invites dormant soul forces to further awaken, results in constructive adjustments of states of consciousness, and empowers us to persist on the spiritual path with unwavering faith in the certain outcome of our dedicated endeavors.

The very best of attainment in this life is to remain
still and let God act and speak through you.
— *Meister Eckhart* —

August 15

Even if the soul's aspiration to be Self-realized is weak, sincere desire to know the reality of God will cause supportive events to unfold to fulfill that desire.

August 16

Whenever you are unable to discern the truth about yourself in relationship to the Infinite, engage in introspective contemplation until your understanding improves. Then continue until you definitely know it.

August 17

When egocentric self-consciousness prevails, it gathers its forces to protect itself against unwanted change or transformation and all of its habits and conditioned characteristics are rallied to its defense. Actively resist these obstacles to soul unfoldment by nurturing devotion to God, intentional right living, and regular meditation practice.

Let your devotion to God be like a wood fire that burns steadily for a long time; not like a straw fire that produces a bright flame and quickly dies out.
— *Paramahansa Yogananda* —

August 18

When your thoughts are irrational and emotions are unsettled, it is difficult to regulate mental and physical impulses. On such occasions, it can be helpful to pray and meditate to infuse the transformational influences of awakened soul awareness into the mind.

August 19

The "ancestors" of desires are egoism and the soul. When egoism is not nourished by attention, it diminishes. When the soul's qualities are nurtured by Self-remembrance, prayer, meditation, and repeated superconscious episodes, only constructive, life-enhancing desires arise in the mind.

August 20

A God-surrendered devotee does not waste energy or time in idle daydreaming, purposeless talk, or useless actions of any kind. Instead, concentrated attention and actions are directed to practices that contribute to psychological transformation and spiritual growth.

Not for anything in the world would I be free
from God; I wish to be free *in* God and *for* God.
— *Nikolai Berdyaev* / *The End of Our Time* —

August 21

When we know that we can choose and immediately assume any state of consciousness at will, we are free from self-defeating beliefs that there are causes external to ourselves that determine or affect our lives.

August 22

Obsessive concern about unimportant matters, and dramatization of addictive mental attitudes and behaviors, are symptoms of egocentric willfulness and emotional immaturity. Be more adventuresome and courageous. Be willing to see the many worthwhile possibilities available to you. Train yourself to be responsible for your mental states and behaviors.

August 23

The awareness of every soul will be fully restored to conscious realization of omnipresence and omniscience. God alone is omnipotent.

The wise person lives after the image of God
and is not guided by the ways of the world.
— *Paracelsus* / *Works* —

August 24

An unenlightened spiritual aspirant's primary obstacle to overcome is tenacious attachment to the erroneous idea that the soul is other than an already perfect expression of God's consciousness. When this error of the intellect is banished, the products of ignorance of the truth cease to be experienced.

August 25

The most efficient way to change unwanted or troublesome mental states and psychological conditions is to determine their causes and remove them. If this cannot easily be done, focused endeavors that will improve mental and emotional states and personal behaviors can and should be implemented.

August 26

To overcome self-centeredness and be relieved of all of the difficulties that are related to this condition, expand your awareness. Choose worthwhile endeavors to which to devote your knowledge, skills, energies, and resources. Be one hundred percent committed to authentic spiritual growth. Invite God to work through you.

I have not so far left the coasts of life to travel inland, that I cannot hear the murmur of the Outer Infinite.
— *Elizabeth Barrett Browning / Aurora Leigh* —

August 27

If resolve for spiritual growth is weak, the deluded mind's self-serving tendencies are inclined to become stronger and more influential. When resolve for spiritual growth is strong and firm, superconscious influences prevail over conflicted psychological states.

August 28

Self-revealed knowledge makes the soul impervious to the effects of mundane causes and spiritual growth is steadily progressive. Obstacles to effective living are then more easily overcome, cease to exist, or are transcended.

August 29

Even a little of our attention and endeavor directed to right living and spiritual practice results in spiritual growth that soon puts the soul into a sympathetic relationship with the currents of evolution and the actions of God's grace. Fear and uncertainty cease.

In the highest state of consciousness you maintain your divine realizations while working, speaking, or moving about in this world. When that state is accomplished, there is no possibility of falling back into delusion.
— *Paramahansa Yogananda* —

August 30

The spiritual aspirant who is not inspired may sometimes practice meditation as a rehearsed ritual that is seldom productive of worthwhile results. To ensure highest benefits, meditate with inspired intention. Remain alert. Let self-consciousness dissolve as conscious awareness of wholeness increases. Desire nothing but to know and realize the reality of God.

August 31

Until the mind is completely illumined and purified, emotions and urges nourished by memories of prior experiences may influence the mind and produce nonuseful desires, fantasies, and hallucinations. These can be resisted, restrained, weakened, and removed by disciplined living and by refined superconscious states which become pronounced when we meditate regularly.

Affirmation

God is my life and I know it.
My purpose in this world is to awaken in God
and I am resolved to do it. Forsaking all things
which are unimportant, I direct my attention
and dedicate myself to God-realization.

Assist Others to Their Highest Good

All souls are aspects of God's consciousness. The fulfillment you desire for yourself, desire for others. Your compassion for others blesses them and you. Pray for the enlightenment and well-being of everyone and for the happiness and well-being of all creatures.

1. What are your wishes for people you know and for everyone on Planet Earth and in all realms?

_____

_____

2. Along with your prayers and good will, what are some of the practical things can you do to assist others to experience well-being and good fortune?

_____

_____

3. What can (and will) you do to protect and nurture the environment and personally contribute to the enlightenment of planetary consciousness?

_____

_____

I acknowledge the innate divine nature of every person.
I am a caring, responsible citizen of the universe.

SEPTEMBER

September 1

When the mind is disciplined by the soul's will and the constructive influences of superconsciousness, and when sense urges have been mastered, subtle impulses which cause mental and emotional transformations are naturally calmed. Soul awareness is then unwavering in the absolute stillness of Self-knowledge.

September 2

Unskilled or overly aggressive endeavors to suppress disturbing thoughts and moods are almost always futile. The effective way to regulate thoughts and emotional states is to act decisively in the course of everyday living and to meditate on a regular schedule.

September 3

Without being influenced by the behaviors or words of others, a devotee of God is always established in Self-knowledge and consistently engaged in right actions.

Thinking that you are not free is what keeps you from demonstrating freedom. Cease from thinking like that and you will be free.
— *Paramahansa Yogananda* —

September 4

When physical and mental restrictions to the free flow of soul awareness are absent, whether one is absorbed in meditative contemplation, involved with activities and relationships, enjoying interludes of leisure, or sleeping, unfoldments of soul qualities are continuous.

September 5

Whenever the currents of evolution are resisted in the field of individualized soul awareness and in the field of planetary consciousness, powerful impulses arise from the omnipresent field of Pure Consciousness to nurture the spiritual awakening and growth of souls and to restore the momentum of evolution.

September 6

Although the true Self is not directly affected either by our habitual actions or by our spiritual practices, its capacities expand and its qualities unfold when supportive actions are implemented to remove physical and mental obstacles which confine and restrict them.

Samadhi [oneness] is experienced when subtle impulses that cause transformations in the individualized field of awareness are returned to their source and made tranquil.
— *Patanjali's yoga-sutras 1:2* —

September 7

In all realms of nature, actions are necessary to produce desired reactions and to remove obstacles to the flows of creative forces. Adjustments of mental states and states of consciousness are actions which can start at subtle and fine levels. They have the most beneficial effects when implemented at the finest level of consciousness.

September 8

Self-realization provides insight into nature's laws of causation that enables us to act from the finest level of consciousness. Here, only mild intention is needed to cause desired effects and to attract supportive events and circumstances that enable purposes to be accomplished.

September 9

Our approach to spiritual growth is more effective when we choose the way which is most compatible with our psychological temperament.

God's wisdom is infinite: it transcends
all our powers of expression.
— *Joseph Alden* / *Conceptions of the Infinite* —

September 10

A problem cannot be satisfactorily solved by the states of consciousness and actions which produced it. To solve problems—including the primary problem of lack of spiritual awareness—learn to see solutions and do what is necessary to manifest them.

September 11

Some people desire a relationship with God because they are in need of healing or improvement of personal circumstances. Some desire only material gain. Some want enough understanding to enable them to have a more satisfying human experience or to provide hope for an afterlife. The wisdom-impelled devotee ardently aspires to complete God-realization. Let wisdom light your way.

September 12

Cosmic perceptions unfold in our awareness when we meditate deeply. The Spirit of God is apprehended as the essence of all souls; the all-pervading reality of God is apprehended as including all souls within itself.

Only for God wait thou in stillness, my soul.
— *The Book of Psalms 62:6* —

September 13

Soul perceptions and experiences during and after transition from the body are determined by one's degree of Self-realization and mental and emotional states. If the departing souls' awareness is not clear and peaceful, subtle mental impulses can disturb the mind and cause confusion. At the time of transition, it is best to be calm and meditative, surrendered to the process with aspiration and gentle intention to awaken to pure consciousness.

September 14

The radiant light of God's consciousness ever shines behind the veils of gross and subtle matter. That light can be perceived and merged with during transition from the body. Devotees who have perceived this light during meditation can easily see and merge with it at will. Daily meditation is the best preparation for the moment of eventual departure from this realm.

The laws of life can teach us how to live in harmony with Nature and with our innate characteristics. When we know what the laws are, and conduct ourselves accordingly, we can live in lasting happiness, good health, and perfect harmony with all life and with ourselves.
— *Paramahansa Yogananda* —

September 15

Always think and speak only about what you want to experience; never mentally dwell on or talk about what you do not want to experience. Avoid gossip. Ignore the faults you see in others. Acknowledge your own innate divinity and look for it in others. Avoid complaining about your personal problems or about circumstances that do not please you. Expand your consciousness. Rally your soul forces. Use your powers of imagination and will. Learn to be problem-free and to always have ideal circumstances.

September 16

When we pray to God, believing God to be a being distinct from us, desires that are possible of being fulfilled can be fulfilled according to our belief and our capacity to accept. It is then not God who fulfills our desire, but ourselves—by assuming a point of view which enables us to perceive and acknowledge the desired outcome. Without belief that results in inner conviction, and acceptance of the conditions for which we pray, our prayers are powerless to be transformative. Most prayers of this kind are not "answered" because the one who prays does not really believe that the desired outcomes are possible.

Direct love toward God and peace comes over the soul. ...
— *Fulton J. Sheen* / *Peace of Soul* —

September 17

Eliminate all nonessentials from your life and focus your thoughts and actions only on what is important. You will then more efficiently accomplish your duties and successfully fulfill your real purpose for being in this world— to awaken to God-realization.

September 18

Be respectful and courteous when in relationship to others while avoiding excessive and unnecessary social interaction. Be ever mindful that behind the facade of every personality, behind the words and deeds of others, is the pure light of God which is the same as your inner reality. Communicate soul to soul.

September 19

The River of Time is swallowing your material life and preparing you for your ultimate freedom in God. Live wisely, remembering your spiritual destiny.

While you are learning to swim in the sea of life,
you can help others learn to swim.
— *Paramahansa Yogananda* —

September 20

Being established in awareness of wholeness, with thoughts always turned Godward, purifies the mind and results in conscious attunement with the Infinite.

September 21

All of our soul qualities can be quickly unfolded by remembering our relationship with the Infinite and by living so that we are always in tune with it and in harmony with its inclinations. These two practices comprise the essence of the spiritual life.

September 22

Our clear awareness of the reality of God can be constant. The consummation of the unfoldment of innate soul knowledge is total comprehension of the truth about God and life's processes. Flawed understanding is only partial truth-consciousness; it should not be tolerated.

I salute the supreme teacher, the Truth, whose nature is bliss; who is the giver of the highest happiness; who is pure wisdom; who is beyond all qualities and infinite like the sky; who is beyond words; who is one and eternal, pure and still; who is beyond all change and phenomena and the silent witness to all our thoughts and emotions. I salute Truth, the supreme teacher.
— *Ancient Vedic Hymn* —

September 23

Constructive desires which, when fulfilled, enhance our lives and allow our awareness to expand, are not detrimental to our spiritual growth. Desires impelled by ignorance and insatiable cravings are definitely harmful. Allow only constructive desires to prevail.

September 24

As a person who is hungry desires food, as a person who is thirsty desires water, as a person who is deprived of air desires to breathe freely, so with similar urgency should desire to know and experience God be compelling.

September 25

When our love for someone is constant, we think of them often. When our love for God is like that, thoughts of God are always present. Loving thoughts of God keep us attuned to God's presence.

It wouldn't help some people to remember their past lives. Even in this lifetime, see how habit-bound many people have become. [Almost] everything they do is predictable. As they grow older, the more settled they become in their ways of thinking, feeling, and behaving. They need an opportunity to forget what they have done and start fresh. For them, with a new beginning there is hope of improvement.

— *Paramahansa Yogananda* —

September 26

All souls are individualized units of God's being and all minds are specialized units of God's Cosmic Mind. Whether you are aware of it or not, you are always in God and, through your mind, have a mutually responsive relationship with God's Mind.

September 27

Until you are firmly established in God-realization, continually remind yourself that you exist in God. Remember that God is not an inaccessible being apart from you. God is expressing as you.

September 28

Until you enjoy a mutually responsive relationship with God's Cosmic Mind, train yourself to think clearly and constructively. Notice when Cosmic Mind is responsive to your thoughts, intentions, desires, and needs. With practice, you will easily discern the inner causes of your experiences and circumstances.

The consciousness of God's presence
is the first principle of religion.
— *Hebrew Proverb* —

September 29

If your goals and projects are clearly defined and you are certain that you want them to manifest, expect Universal Mind to respond in the affirmative and it will. If you cannot clearly define what you want or need, expect Universal Mind to produce circumstances for your highest good and it will. You have a divine right to be healthy, happy, successful, and spiritually awake.

September 30

Believe that you can experience authentic spiritual growth. You are more than worthy of it; you are supposed to be Self-realized and God-conscious. Shift your attention from conditioned human consciousness to your divine condition which already exists. Self-realization cannot be created; it can only be acknowledged and demonstrated. Let it be real to you.

Affirmation

Whenever my path is not clearly discerned, I turn inward until my spirit is refreshed. Inspired anew, I go forward with God as my companion in all that I do.

Be Prosperous

To be prosperous is to easily and enjoyably thrive, flourish, and be successful in every way. When you are open and responsive to life, you have the complete support of nature, can enjoy cooperative relationships, and experience rapid spiritual growth. Be willing to prosper.

1. If some of your mental attitudes, beliefs, and behaviors are restricting the flow of life's prospering actions in your life, identify them and write them here:

_____

2. Immediately replace them with thoughts, feelings, and awareness of affluence: of being in the flow of resources, events, and relationships that will assure your well-being. Cultivate a prosperity consciousness.

3. What else are you doing (and will do) to keep yourself open to prosperity? Include your work, savings and investment program, charitable giving, and all actions which will keep you in the flow of good fortune.

_____

_____

_____

God is the source and substance of my highest good.

OCTOBER

October 1

The spiritual basis of real prosperity is to clearly perceive and wholly comprehend the truth that the universe is an undivided manifestation of cosmic forces emanating from and sustained by God's consciousness.

October 2

Prosperity is real when we are so conscious of God's presence that desires are easily fulfilled and all needs are easily provided for by our own skillful endeavors and the spontaneous actions of God's grace.

October 3

If you are reluctant to be prosperous, analyze your thoughts and feelings to discover why you are denying yourself fulfillment. Replace poverty thoughts and feelings with prosperity ideas, feelings, and actions.

Prosperity does not mean always having what you
want when you want it; it means always having what
you need when you need it.
— *Paramahansa Yogananda* —

October 4

To be prosperous is to experience total well-being: to have what we need for our physical comfort; be mentally, emotionally, and physically healthy; be free from addictive tendencies and behaviors; and to live effectively with meaningful purpose.

October 5

When you think about the near and distant future, do you envision ideal circumstances and freedom of expression, or do you envision unsatisfactory conditions and inability to accomplish purposes? Be a possibility-thinker. Envision your highest good and manifest it.

October 6

Nurture your soul qualities. Enlarge your capacity to easily accept health, happiness, and accomplishment as being natural for you to experience. Nothing external to you can prevent you from being fulfilled.

Beloved, I wish above all things that you may prosper and be in health, even as your soul prospers. I rejoiced greatly when your brothers came and told me of the truth that is in you, and that you walk in the truth.
— *New Testament / 3 John 1:2,3* —

October 7

With the knowledge that the elements and forces of nature comprise everything in this world, learn to relate with natural ease to things and circumstances. Be responsible for your choices and actions. Renounce any fears about having and wisely using resources that are available to you.

October 8

When planning an endeavor, envision the desired outcome as it will be when it is manifested. Perform all actions to support orderly unfoldments of events and circumstances. What you can vividly imagine, believe to be possible, and comfortably accept for yourself, can be experienced by you. Think without limitations.

October 9

Learn to skillfully, efficiently, and effectively manage your time, energies, relationships, money, and personal affairs so that your life is always well-ordered and circumstances are in accord with your choices.

I could show you that whatever you believe with
a concentrated mind can immediately occur.
— *Lahiri Mahasaya* —

October 10

If life seems to be denying you the good fortune you desire, perhaps you are consciously or unconsciously withholding yourself from life. Examine your mental attitudes, emotional states, and behaviors to discover whether or not you are limiting yourself.

October 11

When confused, afraid, anxious, emotionally upset, or overwhelmed by circumstances, turn within. Be still. Meditate in the deep silence until you are calm and able to view your circumstances objectively. Rest to restore your reserves of energy. Pray for inner strength, insight, guidance, and spiritual renewal.

October 12

Remember that all problems and limitations are due to lack of spiritual awareness. Improve your understanding of your real Self in relationship to God. Remind yourself that you are in this world to awaken in God and express your knowledge and abilities.

You of little faith, why did you doubt?
— *New Testament* / *Matthew 14:31* —

October 13

Consciousness is what you are; you are not your mind or physical body. The states of consciousness and mental and emotional states you choose will determine your circumstances, relationships, and actions. What are your choices today? Choose wisely, and prosper.

October 14

Established in awareness of *being*, be assured that you already *have* all that you need for your well-being and fulfillment. Soul contentment, rational thinking, and emotional stability provide a firm foundation for your "house" of personal circumstances.

October 15

If you need healing of any kind, remember that your consciousness of wholeness extends to your mind, body, and personal affairs. Let your consciousness of wholeness be fully expressed as mental, emotional, and physical health, and as wholesome personal relationships and ideal circumstances.

God is in all, all that is, is God. The different forms
of existence are God's myriad manifestations.
— *Kabir* —

October 16

Your mental concepts of what you are will change as insights into your real nature are experienced. Your clear realization of your real nature, when permanent, will prevail over illusional perceptions and ideas. Prefer Self-realization to a mental self-image.

October 17

Redeem your awareness from memories of hardship, traumatic events, failures, and misfortune, and restore it to wholeness by viewing memories dispassionately and nurturing Self-knowledge. Allow nothing that occurred in the past to have power to adversely influence your thoughts or behaviors today.

October 18

When unpleasant memories cause you distress, rest in soul awareness and view them with detachment. If you cannot immediately do this, breathe deeply a few times. Be aware in the moment. Remember your innate divine nature. Anchor your awareness in God.

I [Supreme Consciousness] am the origin of all. From me all creation is emanated. Knowing this, wise devotees, endowed with devotion, constantly meditate on me.
— *Bhagavad Gita 10:8* —

October 19

Just as objects in front of a light cause shadows of the objects to appear, so mental images in our field of consciousness cause the shadows of our circumstances to appear on the screen of space-time. Because thoughts and beliefs are more real than their effects, unwanted circumstances can easily be replaced by ones we desire by adjusting mental states and imagery.

October 20

Because we are presently experiencing what we consciously or subconsciously desire, anticipate, or are willing to accept, we are already flawlessly demonstrating the causative laws of manifestation of our mental states and states of consciousness. To change or improve external conditions, we need only to be more responsible for what we are manifesting.

October 21

If present circumstances and relationships are not satisfactory, why are you accepting them in your life?

[The behavior of one who desires to realize] the kingdom of heaven [spiritual fulfillment] can be compared to a merchant, seeking good pearls: who, when he had found the one pearl of great price, went and sold all that he had, and bought it.
— *New Testament* / *Matthew 13:45,46* —

October 22

If we are unable to live effectively, it is unlikely that we will be able to experience satisfying spiritual growth. A success-attitude, constructive behaviors, and powers of concentration that enable us to proficiently accomplish worthwhile mundane purposes can also enable us to accomplish rapid spiritual growth.

October 23

If you can admit that you do not know, you are already wiser than those who believe that they have knowledge they do not yet possess.

October 24

If we are not prospering—if we are not as healthy, happy, successful, and affluent as we would like to be—it may be that we actually know better than we do; that all we have to do is to appropriately use the knowledge and skills we already have.

A soul free from the tumults of passion is an impregnable fortress in which one may take refuge and defy all the powers of earth to enslave him. He that does not see this must be very ignorant: and he who sees it, and does avail himself of this privilege, must be very unhappy.
— *Marcus Aurelius* / *Meditations* —

October 25

Fulfill all duties and perform all actions cheerfully, skillfully, and attentively. You will develop enhanced powers of concentration, improve your functional abilities, and prepare yourself to be appropriately responsive to any challenge or opportunity.

October 26

Wisely choose your friends and associates. Honor the innate divine nature of everyone while nurturing only intimate personal relationships which are for your highest good and the highest good of others. You have dreams to actualize and a spiritual destiny to fulfill. Provide the most constructive circumstances that will enable you to accomplish your purposes.

October 27

Even in the midst of relationships and activities, you are always alone in the Infinite. No one else can think your thoughts, dream your noble dreams, or actualize your spiritual awakening and enlightenment.

There is always a radiance in the soul ... untroubled like the light in a lantern in a wild turmoil of wind and tempest.
— *Plotinus / Enneads* —

October 28

Always do your best, then let God do the rest. You can do much to help yourself to fulfillment; if you do it, God's grace can and will do what you cannot do.

October 29

Life always provides us with what we ask for and are able to accommodate. If prosperity seems to be avoiding you, perhaps you have not yet asked for it; perhaps you have asked but have not prepared yourself to receive it. Fearlessly ask life for that which you deserve. Expand your capacity to receive.

October 30

Remove all obstacles to fulfillment and you will surely be fulfilled. Obstacles which are too resistant for you to remove, let God remove.

When the soul enters into her Ground, into the innermost recesses of her being, divine powers suddenly pour into her.
— *Meister Eckhart / Sermons* —

October 31

Whether we give to others who are in need the gift of our good will, our soulful prayers, constructive advice and encouragement, practical assistance, financial support or necessary material things, our giving should always be thoughtful, appropriate, and of value to the recipient of our compassionate acts without any thought or desire for personal recognition or reward. The moment we appropriately give is our moment of blessing. It is then that we are in the flow of life's supportive actions. We should always give out of the abundance of our awareness of wholeness, knowing ourselves to be but timely agents of the Higher Power which freely bestows its providential and redemptive healing grace.

Affirmation

The enlivening Spirit of God is freely expressive in
and through me. It illumines my mind, regenerates my
body, removes all restrictions to its flow, inspires me
with creative ideas, empowers my constructive actions,
· and harmoniously arranges all of my circumstances
and relationships. All aspects of my life are now
in divine order.

Affirm and Experience the Truth

It is of practical value and spiritually helpful to write clearly defined affirmations that can cause constructive changes in your mind and consciousness.

1. Write an affirmation that best defines your intuitive sense of certainty about the final outcomes of your committed endeavors and the unfoldments of God's grace. Speak it with conviction, until words cease and you are established in conscious realization.

I am love and only love
matters in the infinite Universe.
Let us be guided by love.

2. Write an affirmation that expresses your aspiration for the highest good of others with whom you share this world. Visualize all souls as being awake in God, fulfilling their purposes and their spiritual destiny.

Love, joy, happiness and
kindness are free to all of us,
whatever we do may these principals
seat in our souls.

In confidence and faith, I speak words of truth.

NOVEMBER

November 1

Some people are inclined to believe their preferred approach to God-realization to be the only way. The various modes of worship and spiritual practice are but outer forms, often determined by cultural influences and psychological temperament; the inner way is that of gradual or sudden emergence of the soul's awareness as mental restrictions are weakened and overcome.

November 2

At the core of all truly inspired religious and enlightenment traditions is the vital essence which empowers the teachings and invites and impels the soul to unfold its innate qualities.

November 3

We can never know the precise moment when we will awaken to God-realization. Be alert and watchful.

... Peace, be still.
— *New Testament / Mark 4:39* —

November 4

Stunted emotional growth is an obstacle to spiritual growth. Inability, or unwillingness, to be responsible for our thoughts and actions results in provincial mental attitudes and inclinations to choose dependent relationships to satisfy immature emotional needs. Emotional maturity is essential for effective living and spiritual growth.

November 5

Conditioned mental attitudes and habits of behavior confine soul awareness and perpetuate meaningless living. Like a disease, these characteristics which are common to the spiritually unawake state, are often nurtured and transmitted from one generation to another.

November 6

The infallible cure for the debilitating "illness" of conditioned human consciousness is Self-knowledge that blossoms into God-realization.

When the truth seeker is established in superconsciousness, meditation practice is natural and spontaneous. Then, even when not meditating, its benefits are enjoyed.
— *Lahiri Mahasaya* —

November 7

A primary cause of difficulties that some devotees have in their endeavors to comprehend spiritual realities and to express soul qualities is attachment to ordinary, conditioned states of consciousness which contracts and confines awareness, dulls the mind, clouds the intellect, and inhibits powers of intuition.

November 8

When our attention is preoccupied with externals, we tend to forget our real nature and to be excessively involved with temporary or unimportant relationships and circumstances. Learn to always be soul-centered while relating to the objective realm. Experience the freedom of unbounded, unconfined, awareness.

November 9

The spiritually awake state is the exact opposite of ordinary, conditioned states of awareness. Practice being awake—alert and insightful—at all times.

The Masters say that the soul has two faces. The highest one always sees God, the lower one looks downward and informs the senses. The higher one is the summit of the soul, it gazes into eternity. It knows nothing about time and body.
— *Meister Eckhart / Sermons* —

November 10

When our faculties of perception are purified, we see all that is good and beautiful. When perceptions are marred because of inattentiveness and preconceived notions, because of blurred perceptions we tend to notice only those conditions which reinforce our delusions.

November 11

Train yourself to perceive with accuracy. Choose to see order, harmony, the inner causes of outer effects, and the many opportunities for learning and growth that life is always providing for you.

November 12

When you are soul-centered and happy, all souls everywhere are benefited by your Self-knowledge and happiness. Let your soul light freely shine.

When the devotee is no longer aware of meditating and is stable in Self-knowledge which is nondual and blissful, a true state of oneness is experienced.
— *Lahiri Mahasaya* —

November 13

The most beneficial way to help others is to first help yourself to be God-realized. Go deeper into God.

November 14

Although the soul is outside of time, when we are yet mind-body identified, time is a determining factor in our lives. Use the time that remains for you in this incarnation to awaken in eternity.

November 15

Some people assert that, as a result of their many years of study of metaphysical principles, their condition is that of a higher level of confusion. Confusion at any level is evidence of unawareness of the truth. Banish unknowingness with real knowledge.

Realize the Self to be distinct from the body, sense organs, mind, faculty of intelligence, and primordial nature; it is the witness of their functions and the ruler of them.
— *Adi Shankara* —

November 16

When tempted to delay or to avoid your spiritual studies and practices, remind yourself of the importance of awakening to Self-knowledge. Arouse your inner forces and exercise your power of soul-will. If you willingly and skillfully do what you know you must do to succeed, failure is an impossibility.

November 17

We need not compare our meditative perceptions or soul unfoldment episodes with those claimed by others; the spiritual path is not a contest.

November 18

Some obvious indications of spiritual growth are peace of mind, a progressively increasing awareness of God's presence, unwavering faith, emotional stability, courage, a cheerful demeanor, freedom from addictive inclinations and behaviors, enhanced appreciation for life and living, and effective performance of constructive actions. Nurture these characteristics.

... I maintain that it is a common error among spiritual persons not to withdraw from outward things from time to time to worship God within themselves ...
— *Brother Lawrence / The Practice of the Presence of God* —

November 19

When we experience obvious shifts of awareness to states which are more clear, we perceive ourselves differently in relationship to the world and to others. Our values and goals may change. Time may be required to become accustomed to new ways of perceiving, thinking, and relating. Learn by practice and experimentation how to adapt to the changes that you experience. Be patient with yourself as you progress.

November 20

As your ego-sense diminishes, learn to accomplish purposes with soul-directed intention. Have more trust in the supportive actions of God's grace.

November 21

When ego-sense is diminished, nothing of real value is lost; everything that is worthwhile is realized.

The first means [to practicing the presence of God]
is to lead a very pure life. The second is remaining very
faithful to the practice of this presence and to the interior
awareness of God in ourselves. We ought always to do
this gently, humbly, and lovingly, without allowing
ourselves to be troubled or worried.
— *Brother Lawrence / The Practice of the Presence of God* —

November 22

Fearlessness is characteristic of one who is devoted to the spiritual path. Most people do not know their past, nor do they know what their future will be like. Believe in your Self. Believe in God. Have confidence in knowing that because God's grace has brought you to your present station in life, it will take you the rest of the way.

November 23

Neither the mind nor the personality have power of their own. God is the only power; it is expressive in the universe and is within you at the core of your being. Therefore, never affirm that you are powerless.

November 24

The aspect of God that attracts souls and unveils their consciousness so that spiritual awakening occurs and liberation is realized is referred to as love. Do not resist it.

For God has not given us the spirit of fear;
but of power, and of love, and of a sound mind.
— *New Testament* / *2 Timothy 1:7* —

November 25

The all-pervading presence of God is knowable and can be vividly experienced. Mental restlessness obscures awareness of the reality of God. Quiet the activities of the restless mind and God will be real to you.

November 26

Because God is expressing as souls, we can never be separated from God. Thoughts and feelings of being apart from God arise because of our flawed understanding and illusions. When we experience a relationship with God it only seems that we are being united with God. In truth, we have always been in God.

November 27

Partial awareness of the reality of God can be discerned by intellectual means. The full reality can be experienced by direct soul perception and realization that transcends both the senses and intellect.

If you pray with devotion, the magnetism of your devotional ardor will attract God's presence into your awareness.
— *Paramahansa Yogananda* —

November 28

Knowledge of God is higher knowledge. Knowledge of the realms of nature is lower knowledge. Higher knowledge is of superior value; it enables the soul to understand God and all categories of cosmic manifestation. Lower knowledge is of practical value. Higher knowledge liberates the soul. Live skillfully and effectively in this world while aspiring to higher knowledge.

November 29

From the very first moment when we became involved with the realm of mind and matter, we were destined to eventually awaken from unconscious identification with it and have our awareness restored to wholeness. Why should we not awaken to wholeness now?

I will again declare that highest and best knowledge
which, having known it, all the sages [enlightened souls]
have awakened to supreme perfection.
— *Bhagavad Gita 14:1* —

November 30

When meditating deeply, during the first stage of awakening to intuitively perceived knowledge, the meditator becomes aware of the mental restrictions which have yet to be removed if further unfoldment is to be experienced. Constructive, concentrated endeavor is then possible. The second stage is experienced when mental restrictions which caused discomfort have been weakened to the extent that they can no longer interfere with endeavors to concentrate. The third stage is higher superconsciousness which makes possible examination of subtle and fine levels of consciousness. The fourth stage is Self-realization which enables the meditator to clearly comprehend the relationship of soul to mind and to internal and external phenomena. At the fifth stage, mental influences no longer cause changes in the meditator's awareness. The sixth stage is God-realization which renders the soul impervious to external influences. At the seventh stage the soul abides in realization of pure being.

Affirmation

Regardless of where I am or what I do, I am always aware of God's presence. Soul-empowered, I am always optimistic and purposeful. Helpful to everyone, I am always cheerful, kind, and appropriately supportive.

Be Awake in God

Our awakening in God can be sudden or it can be progressive. Allow your illusional sense of independent selfhood to diminish so that your awareness can quickly be restored to wholeness. You will become more cosmic conscious, aware of the oneness of life. You will intuitively know that you are a like a bubble in the infinite ocean of God's all-pervading consciousness.

1. Nothing separates us from God. It is only the habit of identifying awareness with mental processes and objective phenomena that causes and sustains the illusion of difference. By intellectual discrimination and superconscious meditation practice you can flawlessly apprehend and directly experience the truth of your being and the full reality of God in this lifetime.

2. Be aware of the presence of God at all times. Whatever you direct your attention to will become more real to you. There is no experience that is more fulfilling than God-awareness.

3. Live wisely, wholesomely, and constructively. Do the best of which you are capable. Your soul qualities will unfold and become increasingly expressive. Your mind will be illumined by your inner radiance. Delusions and illusions will vanish. You will be free.

I am always awake in God.